WELCOME TO YOUR INTERNET!

This book will help you make your very own website on the Internet.

Millions of people use the Internet every day - it's like a huge library of pages about every subject you can imagine.

Now, with your own website, you can tell the whole world what YOU think.

Some web site ideas

Here are some ideas for websites:
- Favourite things (like Pets or Music)
- Good causes (like Save the Whale)
- Hobbies (like Football or Computers)
- Favourite subjects (like Vikings)

MORE IDEAS
Have a look at these websites for more ideas to try:

www.snaithprimary.eril.net

www.nettlesworth.durham.sch.uk

thinkquest.org/pls/html/think.library

www.go-berserk.com

We're going to make a website about Vikings to show you how.

Our Home Page.

Hello.
This site is all about our favourite things

here is a list of things we like:
Ships
Visiting Ireland
Going berserk

VIKINGS ON THE WEB
8 of the 9 countries in the world with the most Internet use are in Scandinavia, where the Vikings come from!

i

Contents

Next, what this book will do for you

Introduction - Before you start!

What you need

Your computer already has what you need:

    1. A web browser (like Internet Explorer)

    2. A text editor (like Notepad)

And now you have this book to help you!

We've used Windows and Internet Explorer, but you can use a Mac or Linux and any browser (visit www.go-berserk.com for instructions).

NOTE
To find Internet Explorer on Windows: Click on "Start", then "Programs" (or "All Programs"), then "Internet Explorer", or find the "e" icon:

To find Notepad on Windows, click on "Start", then "Programs" (or "All Programs"), then "Accessories", then "Notepad", or find the Notepad icon

What this book will do for you

In this book you'll learn how to make web pages. We'll use the best HTML (Hypertext Markup Language) and the coolest CSS (Cascading Style Sheets).

It may sound difficult, but it isn't really... and it'll make you a web genius. Even most university students don't know what you'll know by the end!!

How this book works

So that you can find things easily, all the parts of the book are numbered with capital letters (A, B), then numbers (1, 2), then small letters (a, b). The writing is coloured to help you know what to read.

- You DON'T need to read what's in these boxes (but it is helpful):

FUN FACTS	NOTE	IDEA	CODE
These boxes contain fun Internet facts	These boxes give helpful suggestions	These boxes give you ideas to try	These boxes describe what is happening in the code.

- You DO need to read what is in the main (centre) part of the page.

  Any important code words in the text are coloured yellow.

```
Code we'll write is in dark blue on a white background.
New code is in red, so you can see what's been added.
```

By the end of Chapter 4, you'll have made a good website.
Chapter 5 and the Appendix add amazing effects (but you can ignore them).

- In a **Heading**:

  ⓘ means something is **more difficult**.

  ✕ means something is **not necessary** for your website to work.

Lesson 1 – Make Your First Web Page

Would you like to make your own Internet pages?

By the end of this book you will be able to make pages like this:

Figure 1: web pages you will build

You'll be able to:

- Make pictures move
- Merge colours into each other
- Show videos and pictures on your web site

And more....

In this chapter, you'll learn how to make a page like this:

ANYTHING BUT MY COMPUTER!
In a survey, 1 in 3 children said that the computer was the one thing they could not live without.

IDEA
If you go to the page and click "View" (from the tool bar), then "Source Code", you can see the HTML code that makes the page.

This works with any web page!

Figure 2: chapter 1 completed page

A. STARTING THE PAGE

"New" and "Folder" in menu list

1. Creating the folders for the page

1) Find space on your computer for the web page

2) Create a folder to hold the web page
   a. Right-click in the empty space
      A menu will appear

Figure 3: New Folder menu

   b. Select "New" then "Folder" from the list.
      A folder will appear called "New Folder"
   c. Double-click on the name "New Folder"

   d. Type in a new name, *e.g. "My Website"*

   e. Double-click on the folder picture (or icon)
      The folder will open up.

folder picture

folder name

Figure 4: a new folder

2. Creating the web page

1) Right-click in the empty space in your folder
   Another menu will appear (like Figure 3) .

2) Select "New" then "Text Document"
   A new Text Document will appear.

3) Double-click on the Text Document picture
   The Text Document will open up.

4) Type this into it:

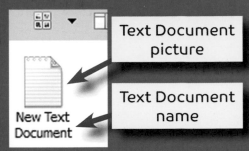

Text Document picture

Text Document name

Figure 5: Text Document

new code is in red

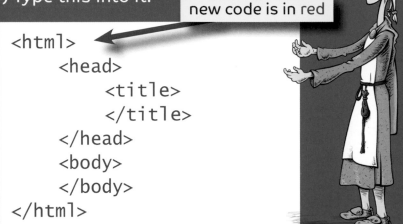

```
<html>
    <head>
        <title>
        </title>
    </head>
    <body>
    </body>
</html>
```

This is the basic code in every Internet page.

NOTES
1. You can write the HTML code in capital letters if you want (e.g. <HEAD>), but it's better to use lowercase letters (<head>).

2. You can use spaces and the Enter key to put the words on new lines (like our code),
or
you can type it without spaces on one line if you want. e.g.
<html><head><title>

(space and new lines are ignored by the computer, so they aren't important).

3. You can put lots of spaces in at once by pressing the Tab key on your keyboard.

a. brackets and words

• The code is made up of words surrounded by brackets (<>), sometimes with a forward slash (/) at the start.

• Every word appears twice, but not in the same order.

The brackets (<>) are put round words to form "tags".
• If a tag has a / before the word it is a closing tag,
• if it doesn't it is an opening tag.

TOP WEB COUNTRIES
The only country in the world where everyone is online is the Falkland Islands (with a population of 2,408 people)

b. pairs and containers

Tags usually come in pairs.

• You can see that every opening tag (e.g. <html>) has a closing tag (e.g. </html>).

• You can also put tags inside other tags, like boxes inside boxes (e.g. the <head> tags contain the <title> tags).

Next, open the web page

c. good-looking code

To make the code look nicer, we've used spaces to:

- put each tag on a new line,
- line up pairs of tags,
- and show which tags contain which.

But you can write the code without any spaces, all on the same line.

The computer just ignores spaces.

3. Saving as a web page

Before we fill in the page with other things, you'll need to save it as an HTML page so that the computer knows to open it as a web page.

1) In the text document's menu (along the top), click on "File"

   The File Menu will appear with lots of options.

2) Click on "Save As" (NOT "Save")

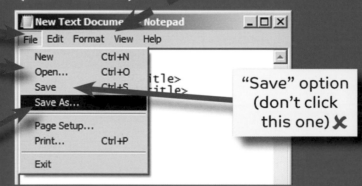

"File" button

"File" menu

"Save As" option (click this one)

"Save" option (don't click this one) ✗

Figure 6: File, Save As menu

The "Save As" box appears.

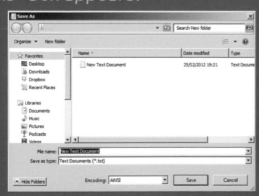

Figure 7: Save As box

IDEA
If you name the first web page in a web site index.html (with a small i), it will help the computer find the page.
Make sure you call it index.html NOT Index.html (with a capital I)

3) Type in the name you want to call the page in the "File name" box.

   We'll call our page "index".

   Make sure you type .html after the name, *e.g. index.html.*

   This will tell the computer that it is a web page.

4) Change the "Save as type:" to "All files" by clicking on the drop-down list and selecting it

5) Click on Save

The computer will now save the file as an html file.
If you want to save any more changes to the page you can just click on "File" then "Save" in the text file's menu bar at the top of the text file.

4. Opening the web page

You can see in your folder that the file has a web page picture on it.
This picture could be a picture from the browser you use to open web pages, or a globe. On Windows, it's usually a blue Internet Explorer "e".

NOTE
You may see two files in the folder, the web page and a Text Document with the same name as the web page (Text Documents look like Figure 5). You can delete the Text Document. You only need the web page.

web page called "index" in the "My Website" folder

Figure 8: the web page in the folder

This file has two parts to it – the outside part which you see on the Internet, and an inside part where the html code is. It's a bit like a human body, where all your insides shape what your outsides look like.

a) To see the web page as it will be on the Internet, double click on it.

web page called "index" displayed in a browser

THE FIRST WEB PAGE
You can see the first web page ever here:
www.w3.org/
History/19921103-
hypertext/hypertext/
WWW/TheProject.html
Lots of links, no colour and no pictures.
It was browsed by the first surfer, the Belgian Robert Cailliau.

Figure 9: index.html opened in Internet Explorer

Next, put things onto the page

b) To see the HTML code inside the web page:

1. Go to your folder (see page 5) and right-click on the web page

2. Select "Open With" then "Notepad"

The code page will appear in a Notepad window.

HTML
HTML stands for "Hypertext Markup Language". It's a computer language made up of tags (markup). Hypertext is links to other pages.

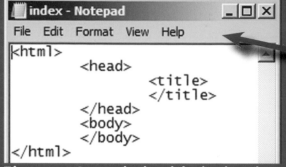

the code page of your web page "index.html" open in Notepad

Figure 10: code inside index.html

At the moment, the page hasn't got any text or pictures in it.

NOTE
If Notepad doesn't appear in the "Open With" menu:
1. Click on "Choose Default Program" or "Choose Program"
   The "Open With" window will appear.
   A. If Notepad is in the "Recommended Programs" or "Other Programs" list, click on it
   Otherwise:
   B. Click on "Browse"
      a. Browse to "Computer", then "C:", then "Windows" or "WINNT", then "System32", then click on "Notepad"
      b. Click "Open"
The code page will open, and Notepad will appear in the "Open With" menu next time.

"Browse" button

Notepad in "Recommended Progams"

B. PUTTING THINGS INTO THE PAGE

1. Adding a Title (using title)

Anything you write between the <title> and </title> tags will appear in the title bar of the web page.

1) Make sure you are in the HTML code of the web page

   a. Go to the code page by clicking on the page's icon in your toolbar at the bottom of the computer screen

   It will have a grey box icon, and will be called "index – NotePad" if you hover your mouse over it.

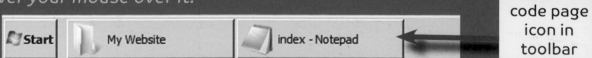

code page icon in toolbar

Figure 11: code page in the toolbar at the bottom of the screen

2) Give the page a title by typing it in between the opening and closing Title tags, <title> and </title>

We've chosen "Home Page" as our title.

```
<title>Home Page
</title>
```

new code is in red

code you've already written is in blue

3) Click on "File" then "Save:" in the text file menu to save the changes

4) Go to the web page

If you have already opened the web page then:

a. Click on the web page's icon in your toolbar at the bottom of the

web page icon in toolbar

Figure 12: web page in toolbar at the bottom of the screen

It will have the icon of your browser (e.g. "e" for Internet Explorer). If you hover your mouse over the icon, it will have the same name as the title of the page followed by the name of your browser.

If you have not opened the web page (or you have closed it) then:

b. Go to the folder where the web page is, and double-click on it (see above on page 5)

5) Click on the Refresh or Reload button (usually 1 or 2 curved arrows)

the title 'Home Page' in the top of the window

the title on the page's tab

refresh button

NUMBER 1 WEB BROWSER
The first web browser was built in 1991 by Nicola Pellow, an undergraduate maths student. You can see a picture of it here: info.cern.ch/www20/photos

Figure 13: the web page with a title

You can now see the changes on the web page.
- *The top of the page is now called "Home Page".*
- *If the browser has tabs (like Figure 13), the title will appear on a tab.*

Next, write on the page

2. Writing on the page (in the body)

Anything you write between the <body> and </body> tags will appear in the web page.

1) Follow steps 1 to 5 (on pages 6 and 7), except instead of typing something between the <title> tags, type it between the <body> tags, e.g.

```
<body>
     Our Home Page. Hello. This site is all about our
favourite things
</body>
```

When you refresh the page (step 5) you will see what you have written:

WARNING
Make sure you never put your address, phone number, email or contact details on your website - you never know who might try to contact you.

Figure 14: writing in the body of the page

3. Writing on different lines (using p)

If you want to have the sentences on different lines, you can use <p> tags.
1) Open up the code page

new code is in red

code you've already written is in blue

2) Change the text in the body tags to read:

```
<p>Our Home Page.</p>
<p>Hello. This site is all about our favourite things</p>
```

3) Save the code by clicking on "File" then "Save" in the Notepad code page

4) Click on the Refresh button on the web page to refresh it

WEB LINGO
In 1965 Ted Nelson came up with the idea of pages that could link to other pages - he called them Hypertext (which is the HT in HTML)

Figure 15: text on new lines using the p tags

The "Our Home Page." is on one line, the "Hello. This site is all about our favourite things" is on another, and a space has now appeared between the two lines.

4. Writing on different lines (using br)

If you don't want spaces between lines, use the <br /> tag:

1) Open up the code page

2) Change the text in the body tags to read:

```
<p>Our Home Page.</p>
<p>Hello.<br />This site is all about our favourite
things</p>
```

CODE
br stands for break. It only needs one tag <br />. Unlike <p>...</p>, there are no closing <br /> tags.

3) Refresh the web page and you will see this:

IDEA
If you type <hr /> instead of <br />, you will get a horizontal line, like this:

Hello. _____
This site is all about

This works with any web page!

Figure 16: text on new lines using the br tag

The "Hello" and "This site is all about.." are on separate lines, but there is no big space between the lines.

Let's add some more lines for practice. We'll make a list of some of our favourite things:

4) Add this under favourite things</p>

```
this site is all about our favourite things</p>
<p>here is a list of things we like:<br />
Ships<br />
Visiting Ireland<br />
Going berserk<br />
</p>
```

5) Save the code and refresh the web page
You'll see the new lines in the code put on new lines on the page.

C. ADDING SOME COLOUR (USING body)

You can colour the whole page (and the writing on it) by typing colours inside the <body> tag.

1) Open the code, and change the first body tag to this:

```
<body bgcolor="yellow" text="blue">
```

CODE
bgcolor stands for Background colour.
It colours the whole body tag (i.e. the whole page).
text colours all the writing in the body tag.

2) Save the code and refresh the web page

WEIRD NOTE
Only use straight speech marks (like "...") not curly ones (like "..."). HTML doesn't like curly speech marks.

To make sure you use straight ones, always type your speech marks in the code page using Notepad.

(beware: if you copy code from Word, for example, it'll make all the straight speech marks curly)

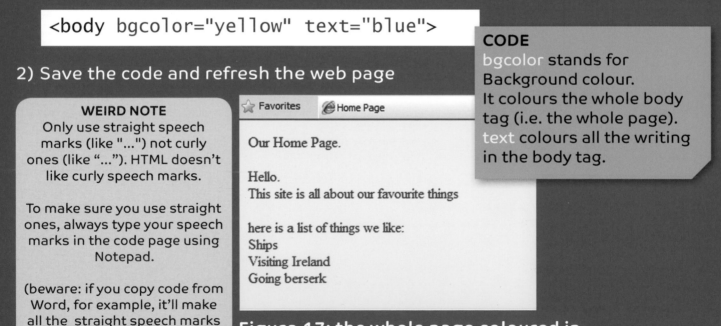

Figure 17: the whole page coloured in

The whole page is coloured yellow, and the text on the page is blue.

You can replace the "yellow" and "blue" colours for almost any colour that you can imagine.

There are a huge number of colours. The 16 basic ones are:

black	navy	blue	green	teal	lime	aqua	maroon
purple	olive	gray	silver	red	fuschia	yellow	white

Table 1: the 16 basic colours

There are 124 other ones from:

AliceBlue though OrangeRed, Orchid and PaleGoldenRod to YellowGreen.

You can see the complete list at www.go-berserk.com/htmlcolours.html (or on page 62).

Just change the "yellow" or "blue" in the code for the colour you want.

CODE

Your code will now look like this:

COLOUR CLASH
The Internet and Windows computers don't agree over the names of colours. For example, a Windows window coloured gray is actually what the Internet calls silver.

```
<html>
    <head>
        <title>Home Page
        </title>
    </head>
    <body bgcolor="yellow" text="blue">
        <p>Our Home Page.</p>
        <p>Hello.<br />
        This site is all about our favourite things</p>
        <p>here is a list of things we like:<br />
        Ships<br />
        Visiting Ireland<br />
        Going berserk<br />
        </p>
    </body>
</html>
```

Figure 18: Chapter 1 code

Next, add more colour

In this chapter, we'll add more colour to the page:

NOTE
HTML is written in American so you need to spell things in the code the American way - like color instead of colour and center instead of centre.

GOOGLE'S FIRST NAME
When Google started in 1996, it was called Backrub

Figure 19: Chapter 2 page

We have put other tags and text between opening and closing tags, but you can also put things inside an opening tag.
These 'things' are called parameters, and change what a tag does.

A. CHANGING THE LOOK OF TEXT

1. Colouring text (using font color)

You can put this code round text you want to colour:

```
<font color="green" size="3"> and </font>
```

parameters

1) Open the code page

2) Find the text "Hello." and change it to this:

```
<font color="red" size="3">Hello.</font>
```

parameters

CODE
- color changes the colour of the writing in the <font> tags. You can use any colour (not just "green").
- size changes the size of the writing. "1" is small, "7" is huge (see later on).

You need to use size and color together to change the writing colour.

3) Save the code, go to the web page and refresh it to see the change

The writing (or text) has been coloured red.

FONT FACTS
Not all computers have all fonts on them. Most have Times New Roman, Arial and Verdana, so it's better to use these fonts.
If a computer hasn't got a particular font, it will use Times New Roman.
You can see a list of good fonts to use in the Appendix.

Figure 20: some text coloured red with font color

2. Changing the font of text (using font face)

Text is written in fonts, like "Verdana", or "Arial", which change the way the letters look. Here are the names of some fonts, written in their font:

Times New Roman, Arial, Comic Sans MS, Verdana, **Impact**, ✈︎✂︎■〽︎ ☞✂︎■〽︎◆ (Wing Dings)

To change the font text use the <font> tags with face="font name"

1) Open the code page

another parameter

2) Find the text "Hello" and change the font tag to this:

```
<font color="red" size="3" face="Jokerman">Hello.</font>
```

3) Save the code, go to the web page and refresh it to see the change
The font of the text has changed.

Next, change the shape of the writing   13

COLOUR CLASH
Very strangely, HTML's gray colour is actually darker than its darkgray colour.

Figure 21: the font has changed with font face

You can make the font bigger or smaller using the size parameter. size="7" is huge, size="1" is very small.
But a better way to change the size is to use the heading tags (e.g. <h1>).

3. Changing the font of all the text using style

If you want to change the font of all the writing on the page, type this into the <body> tag: style="font-family: First Font, Second Font"

1) Open up the code page

> this is CSS code - we'll learn about it later on

2) Find the body tag and change it to this:

```
<body style="font-family: Arial, Serif"
bgcolor="yellow" text="blue">
```

3) Save the code, go to the web page and refresh it

The font of all the writing on the page has changed (except for "Hello",
because it is changed by the <font> tag).

CODE
The page will try to write the text in the First Font (Arial).

If the computer doesn't have that font, it will try the Second Font (Serif).

If it doesn't have that one, it will use Times New Roman.

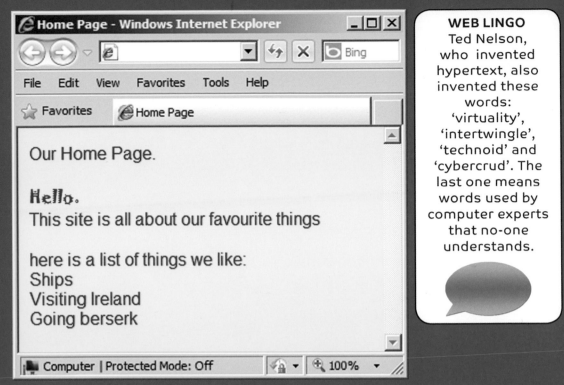

Figure 22: the rest of the text has changed font with style

4. Make writing big or small (using h1)

To make writing bigger, put it between <h1> and </h1> tags.

1) Go to the code page (see step b on page 6)

2) Change the <p> tags round "Our Home Page" to <h1> tags like this

```
<h1>Our Home Page.</h1>
```

*The code between the body tags down to the list will look like this
(I've put some of the code on new lines to make it easier to see):*

```
<body style="font-family: Arial, Serif" bgcolor="yellow"
text="blue">
    <h1>Our Home Page.</h1>
    <p>
        <font color="red" size="3"
        face="Jokerman">Hello.</font><br/>
        This site is all about our favourite things
    </p>
    <p>here is a list of things we like:<br />
```

3) Now save the code page, go to the web page and refresh to see the changes (see steps 3, 4 and 5 on page 6)

The words "Our Home Page" will look much bigger because they are surrounded by <h1> tags.

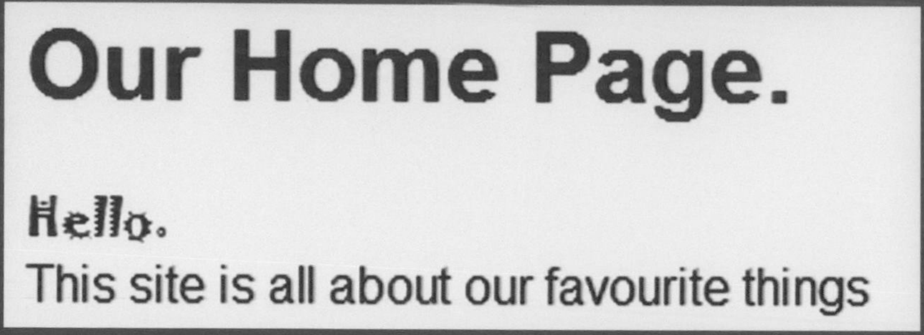

Our Home Page.

Hello.
This site is all about our favourite things

Figure 23: h1 heading tags

You can also use <h2> to <h6> tags in the same way.

Here is what writing in heading tags looks like:

writing between h1 tags

writing between h2 tags

writing between h3 tags

writing between h4 tags

writing between h5 tags

writing between h6 tags

> **IDEA**
> Try some of these tags:
>
> <small> and <big> make writing smaller and bigger.
>
> <sub> puts writing in subscript - like this
>
> <super> puts writing in superscript - like this.
>
> Don't forget the closing tags, like this:
> <small>tiny</small>

B. CENTRE AND EMPHASISE TEXT

1. Emphasise text with Italic (i), Bold (b) and Underline (u)

*The <i> tag makes text italic, <b> makes text **bold** and <u> underlines text.*

1) Go to the code page

2) Before the "this site is all about my favourite things" type in <u><b><i>, and after it type in the closing tags </i></b></u>

The code will look like this:

```
<font color="red" size="3" face="Jokerman">Hello.</font><br />
<u><b><i>This site is all about our favourite things
</i></b></u>
```

3) Save the code, go to the web page and refresh it

You will see this:

Figure 24: <i>, <b> and <u> tags

NOTE
You have to put tags within tags.
<b><i>Hi</i></b>
will work. The <i> tags are inside the <b> tags.

<b><i>Hi</i></b>

But <b><i>Hi</b></i>
will NOT work because the closing </b> tag is inside the closing </i> tag.

<b><i>Hi</b></i>

2. <u>Centre text (using align)</u>

You can put align="center" in heading or p tags, like this:
<p align="center">

align puts the text on the left, right or centre of the page. We've made the parameter align equal to center (which puts the text in the centre).

Let's centre all the text we've written so far.

1) Open the code page (see step 1 on page 6)

COLOUR CONFUSION
If you colour something grey (color="grey") it will actually go green in older Internet Explorer browsers! They don't recognise grey and think you mean <u>green</u>. For grey you have to use the American spelling "gray".

2) Find the <p> tag before "here is a list" text and put this inside it:

```
<p align="center">here is a list of things we like:<br />
```

3) Now do the same thing for the other <p> tag, and the <h1> tag so that the code now looks like:

```
<h1 align="center">Our Home Page.</h1>
<p align="center">
    <font color="red" size="3" face="Jokerman">Hello.</font><br />
    <u><b><i>This site is all about our favourite things</i></b>
</u>
</p>
<p align="center">here is a list of things we like:<br />
    Ships<br />
    Visiting Ireland<br />
    Going berserk<br />
</p>
<p align="center">here is a list of things we like:<br />
```

4) Save the code, go to the web page and refresh it. (see 3-5 on page 6)
The writing "Home Page" will now start in the middle of the page.

VAGUE BUT EXCITING
When Tim Berners-Lee suggested the idea of HTML, his boss (Mark Sendall) called it "vague but exciting". See the original drawing at info.cern.ch/ Proposal.html

Figure 25: all the writing in the middle of the page

CODE

Your code will now look like this:

```html
<html>
    <head>
        <title>Home Page
        </title>
    </head>
    <body bgcolor="yellow" text="blue">
        <h1 align="center">Our Home Page.</h1>
        <p align="center">
            <font color="red" size="3" face="Jokerman">
                Hello.
            </font><br />
            <u><b><i>
                This site is all about our favourite things
            </i></b></u>
        </p>
        <p align="center">
            here is a list of things I like:<br />
            Ships<br />
            Visiting Ireland<br />
            Going berserk<br />
        </p>
    </body>
</html>
```

Figure 26: Chapter 2 code

BROWSER WARS: ATTACK OF THE TAGS
In 1995, to get people to use Internet Explorer, MIcrosoft produced the <marquee> tag which moves things across the screen. Netscape hit back with the <blink> tag that made writing flash.

BROWSER WARS II: REVENGE OF THE BLINK
In the Internet Explorer / Netscape war, Internet Explorer's <marquee> tag still works (and we'll use it). Netscape's <blink> doesn't work any more. But... Netscape became Firefox and is now the world's most popular browser.

We are getting on very well!

Next, pictures and links

In this chapter, we'll add pictures and links to other pages:

Figure 27: Chapter 3 pages

You can put other things into the web page like pictures and links to other web pages. Both of these use other files.

A. ADDING PICTURES

1. Creating a folder for the pictures

To add a picture, it is easier to put the picture in a place close to the web page. We need to create a folder called "images" next to the web page:

1) Go to the folder which contains the web page

2) Right-click in the folder and choose "New" then "Folder"

3) Name the folder "images"

GOOGOL
The founders of the search engine Google named it after a Googol (1 followed by 100 0s). Unfortunately, they spelled the number wrongly.

Figure 28: images folder

2. Getting a picture for the web page

1) Go onto the Internet and search for a picture you want on your page

2) Right-click on the picture and choose "Save As"

3) Browse to the folder you created called "images" and choose "Save"
The picture will be saved to the images folder.
We have saved a picture called "picture.gif "into the images folder.

3. Finding the picture's full name

Computers add three letters to the end of a picture's name so that they know what type of picture it is – this is the picture's full name.
You need to know the full name to add the picture to the web page.

1) Right click on the picture

2) Select "Properties"
The Properties box will appear.
You will need to find specific things in the box.
We'll use them to put the picture on the page.

Chapter 3 – Pictures and Links

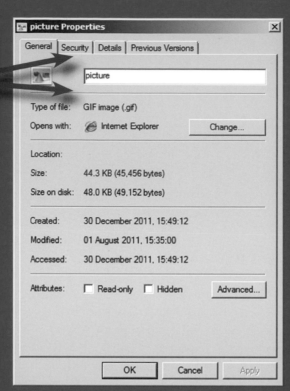

the full name of the picture, including the three letter code, is "picture.gif"

Figure 29: Properties box for a picture

The name of the picture that you need to use is in the box at the top.

Here is a table which lists the most common picture formats.
It gives their three letter codes (called file extensions) and some comments to help you decide which to use.

Format	3 letter code	Good?	Comments
GIF (Graphic Interchange Format)	.gif e.g. picture.gif	✓✓✓	very popular. it is very small, and allows moving pictures but is not the best quality
JPG (Joint Photographic Group)	.jpg, jpeg e.g. picture.jpg	✓	good quality but can be very large
BMP (Bit Map Picture)	.bmp e.g. picture.bmp	✗	not good quality, large, may not display in some browsers
PNG (Portable Network Graphics)	.png e.g. picture.png	✓✓	good quality, can be large

Table 2: picture file formats

4. Adding the picture to the web page

*You need to use the **img** tag (short for IMaGe). It's like the **br** tag, because it doesn't need an end tag –*
just <img /> is enough, NOT <img>...</img>.

*The **img** tag has a parameter called **src** (for SouRCe) which you fill in with the name of the picture and the folders that the web page has to open to get to it, like this: "folder/file".*

1) Open the code page
Let's put a picture after "Going berserk".

2) After the last </p> tag, type in this:

```
here is a list of things I like:<br />
    Ships<br />
    Visiting Ireland<br />
    Going berserk<br />
</p>
<p>
    <img src="images/picture.gif" alt="Us" />
</p>
```

NOTE
1. A forwardslash (/) not a backslash (\) in the src.
2. The picture's full name (including the 3 letter code).
3. The picture's exact name, including capital letters if there are any – so in this case picture.gif NOT Picture.gif.
4. Straight speech marks (")!
5. The img tag has a final />.

3) Save the code, and refresh the web page
The picture has been put into the page.

NOTE
Moving pictures are called 'Animated Gifs'. You can search for these pictures online and download them for your web page by typing 'animated gif' into a Google search.

CODE
The <img /> tag's alt parameter is what appears if the web page can't show the picture. It usually describes what's in the picture.

The src parameter tells the web page which folders to open to get to the picture file. Our web page needs to open the images folder to get to picture.gif (so src="images/picture.gif").

If the picture.gif file was in the same folder as the webpage the src would be "picture.gif".

Figure 30: a picture in the page

If you look closely the picture has flashing eyes- it's a moving picture!! (A simpler way of getting any picture to move is described on page 37).

Next, make a picture fill the page

5. Making the picture bigger or smaller

To make the picture bigger or smaller, you can add the height and width parameters and a percentage (%).
100% is normal size, 200% is twice the size and 50% is half size.

We need to make the picture half the size (50%), because it's too big.
1) Open the code page

2) In the img tag, type in this:

```
<img src="images/picture.gif" alt="Us" height="50%" width="50%" />
```

3) Save the code, go to the web page and refresh it to see what happened
   The picture is now half the size it was.

4) Now let's add in another picture next to it, with this code
   We've saved another picture called "vikship.gif" next to "picture.gif".

```
<img src="images/vikship.gif" alt="ship" height="40%" width="40%" />
<img src="images/picture.gif" alt="Us" height="50%" width="50%" />
```

NOTE
1. There are speech marks round 50% and 40% in the code.
2. And they're straight speech marks (")!
3. You might have to change the numbers to make the pictures fit next to each other.

Figure 31: the picture made smaller and another added

BROWSER WARS III: A NEW HOPE
By 1997 some browsers were allowing some HTML tags, and others weren't. Then came Wilbur – a type of HTML that all the browsers agreed on. Most web pages are written in Wilbur.

B. ADDING BACKGROUND PICTURES

You can make a picture repeat across the whole page by using the background parameter in the body tag, for example, <body background="picture.gif">.

Let's create another web page and put a background image on it.

1) Follow steps A.2.1 to A.2.4 on page 3 to create a new web page
   a. call the page ships.html and save it (as described on page 4)
   b. open up the code in the page (as described on page 6)

2) Get a picture for the background from the Internet and save it to the "images" folder (as described on page 21)
   We have saved a picture of the sea called "IrishSea.jpg".

3) Between the <title> tags type:

```
<title>Ships</title>
```

4) In the <body> tag type this:

```
<body background="images/IrishSea3.jpg">
    <h1>Ships</h1>
```

5) Save the code, go to the web page and refresh it to see what happened

```
<html>
    <head>
        <title>Ships
        </title>
    </head>
    <body background="images/IrishSea3.jpg">
        <h1>Ships</h1>
    </body>
</html>
```

The picture is repeated across the entire page

NOT MYSPACE
A recent survey found one quarter of all 8 to 12 year olds had a page on Facebook, MySpace or Bebo, even though the age limit is 13!!!

... and one in three 5 to 7 year olds have used Facebook.

Next, make links to other pages

THE TAG THAT STARTED IT ALL
Before HTML no page had links to any others. Then HTML introduced the <a> tag which adds links to other pages...and the web was born.

<a>...

Figure 32: a background picture

C. ADDING LINKS TO OTHER PAGES

1. Links to other web sites

You can make a link on a page to another web page. When you click on the link, you will be taken to the new web page.

For example <a href="http://www.google.com">link</a> makes a link that goes to the Google page. The <a> tag makes the link, and the href parameter tells you where the link goes to.

1) Go to the code on the index.html page

2) Before the end body tag (</body>), round the "Visiting Ireland" text this:

```
<a href="http://www.discoverireland.com">Visiting Ireland</a>
<br/ >
```

3) Save the code, go to the web page and refresh it

A link has appeared at the bottom of the page – "Visiting Ireland" is now blue and underlined. If you click on it, you'll go to the Discover Ireland web page.

NOTE
1. You can change the href parameter to any web page.
2. You need to put http:// before a web page address on a website that isn't your own.

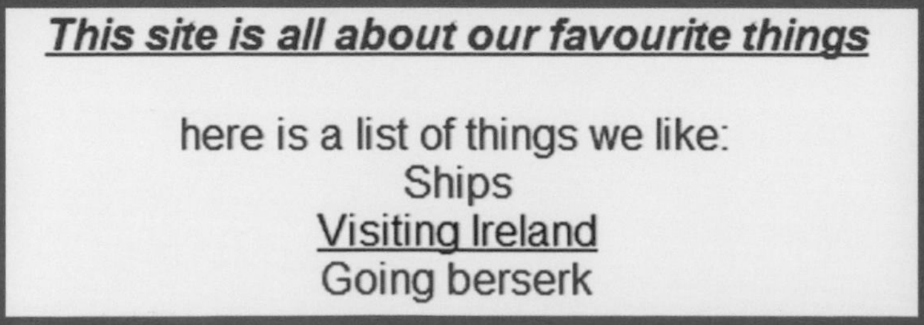

This site is all about our favourite things

here is a list of things we like:
Ships
Visiting Ireland
Going berserk

Figure 33: links to the Internet

2. Links to your web pages

1) On the index.html page, in the code add this around the ships text:

```
<a href="ships.html">Ships</a><br />
```

2) Save the code, go to the web page and refresh it

There is a new link at the bottom of the page.
If you click on it, you will be taken to ships.html.

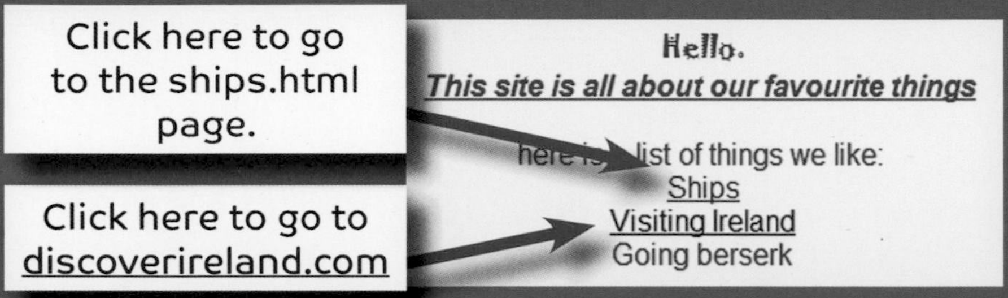

Click here to go to the ships.html page.
Click here to go to discoverireland.com

Hello.
This site is all about our favourite things

here is a list of things we like:
Ships
Visiting Ireland
Going berserk

Figure 34: links to your web pages

NOTE
1. You need to type the name of the web page exactly – including the capital letters. In this case ships.html will work but Ships.html may not.
2. Make sure to put straight speech marks ("...") round the web page name.
3. The ships.html page is in our website, so we don't need the http:// part.

CODE
The href parameter is like the `<img />` tag's src parameter. It tells the web page which folders to open to get to the new page.

our index.html page is in the same folder as the new page, (so href="ships.html").

- If the ships.html file was in the "images" folder next to the index.html page the href would be images/ships.html

- if the ships.html file was in a new folder called "pages" in the "images" folder the href would be images/pages/ships.html

How are you doing?

3. Adding Comments to HTML Code

Sometimes it's useful to add comments to HTML code:
- *comments remind you what the code does,*
- *but the computer ignores them*

1) Open the page and add these comments to the Ships link

```
<a href="ships.html">Ships</a><!--cool!--><br />
```

The comments are between the **<!-- -->** *code.*

2) Save the page and refresh it
The computer ignores the comments!

Next, all the code put together

CODE
Here is the code for index.html and ships.html:

index.html

```
<html>
    <head>
        <title>Home Page
        </title>
    </head>
    <body bgcolor="yellow" text="blue">
        <h1 align="center">Our Home Page.</h1>
        <p align="center">
            <font color="red" size="3" face="Jokerman">Hello.
            </font><br />
            <u><b><i>This site is all about our favourite things
            </i></b></u>
        </p>
        <p align="center">here is a list of things we like:<br />
            <a href="ships.html">Ships</a><!--cool!--><br />
            <a href="http://www.discoverireland.com">Visiting
                Ireland</a><br />
            Going berserk<br />
        </p>
        <p>
            <img src="images/vikship.gif" alt="ship"
            height="40%" width="40%" />
            <img src="images/picture.gif" alt="Us" height="50%"
            width="50%" />
        </p>
    </body>
</html>
```

> **<a> WEB PAGE <img /> IDEA**
> you can put any web page inside a web page by using the <iframe> tag!
> *This will put ships.html into a page:*
> <iframe src="ships.html" width="100px" height="100px"></iframe>
>
> It's like the <img /> tag beause it uses src, width and height. The height and width say how big the <iframe> is in pixels (like millimetres) ..but the src is like the <a> tag's href - it uses a web page name; and <iframe> needs a closing </iframe> tag.

ships.html

```
<html>
    <head>
        <title>Ships</title>
    </head>
    <body background="images/IrishSea3.jpg">
    </body>
</html>
```

> **NOTE**
> The <a> tag puts the H in HTML. The tag makes links which experts call "hyperlinks".
> This hyper makes HTML "Hypertext Markup Language".

Figure 35: Chapter 3 code

In this chapter we'll show you how to add tables and make pictures move:

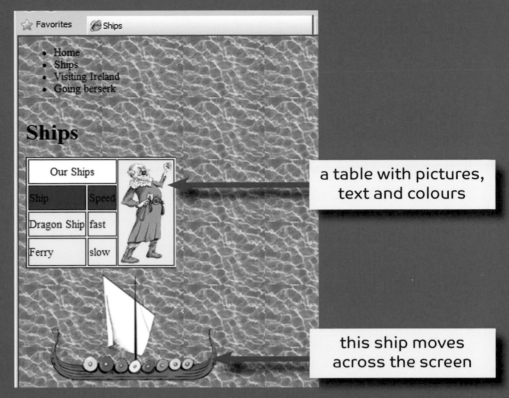

a table with pictures, text and colours

this ship moves across the screen

Figure 36: Chapter 4 pages

A. TEAM TAGS - MAKE LISTS USING li

We have seen that some tags come in pairs (like <font> and </font>) and others work alone (like <img />). However, some tags need to work with others to do things. These are "team tags".

1. Making lists (using ol, ul and li team tags)

The ul and ol tags make lists from text, but they need li tags to help them.

- *ul (for Unordered List) puts bullet points before each item (like this list).*

  This list has bullet points (like a ul list)

- *ol (for Ordered List) numbers the items in the list.*

- *li tags (for List Item) go round each item in the list.*

1) Go to the code on the ships.html page

This list is numbered (like an ol list)

2) After the opening <body> tag type in:

```
<body background="images/IrishSea3.jpg">
     <ul>
          <li>Home</li>
          <li>Ships</li>
          <li>Visiting Ireland</li>
          <li>Going berserk</li>
     </ul>
<h1>Ships</h1>
```

<a> SMALL FORTUNE, (JUST NOT YET)
The original idea for hyperlinks (in <a> tags) was that every time you clicked on a link to a page, the page's author would get a (very small) sum of money.

<a>

3) Save the code page, go to the web page and click on refresh
The list has bullets in front of each item, like this:

- *Home*
- *Ships*
- *Visiting Ireland*
- *Going berserk*

YOUNGEST COMPUTER EXPERT
Jorge Ospina, aged 15, is the youngest ever computer expert. He is very close to achieving a CCIE certification, which only 20, 000 other (much older) people in the world have.

Figure 37: lists

WARNING!!
Make sure you don't put your address, phone number, email or contact details on your website.
You never know who might use them to contact you.

If you change the ul into ol in the code, the list will now be numbered:

1. *Home*
2. *Ships*
3. *Visiting Ireland*
4. *Going berserk*

B. ADDING TABLES ⓘ

tables are a bit tricky

You can use tables in your pages to make sure text stays in the right place on the page. A table looks like this:

	Left Column (A)	Right Column (B)
Top Row (1)	A1	B1
Bottom Row (2)	A2	B2

Table 3: example table

Instead of A1, B1 etc, you can put anything inside the table: pictures, text, backgrounds or colours. So it is very useful for arranging a page.

Tables are made up of Team Tags (just like the lists above), except they need three sets of tags to work:

1. <table> and </table> are used to make the table
2. <tr> and </tr> are used to make rows in the table (for example, the Top and Bottom Rows in Table 3). tr stands for Table Row.
3. <td> and </td> are used to make cells in each row (for example, the cells A1 and B1 in the Top Row in Table 3). td stands for Table Data.

Here is Table 3 written in HTML:

```
<table>
    <tr>
        <td>A1</td><td>B1</td>
    </tr>
    <tr>
        <td>A2</td><td>B2</td>
    </tr>
</table>
```

Figure 38: a table in HTML

WHITE HATS
People who know how to attack computers using the Internet are called hackers. "Black Hat" hackers cause damage, and "White Hat" hackers try to stop them. They're named after hats because in old cowboy films the good guys always wore white hats and the bad guys always wore black hats.

Next, colour the table

Chapter 4 – Lists, Tables and Moving Pictures

1. Making a table

1) Go to the code of ships.html

2) Under the closing </h1> tag, type in table tags:

```
<h1>Ships</h1>
<table>
</table>
</body>
```

3) Between the table tags, type in two rows, using tr tags

```
<table>
    <tr>
    </tr>
    <tr>
    </tr>
</table>
```

4) In each table row, type in two cells, using td tags

```
<table>
    <tr>
        <td></td><td></td>
    </tr>
    <tr>
        <td></td><td></td>
    </tr>
</table>
```

Let's put some words into the table:

5) In the <td> cells type in this

```
<tr>
    <td>Dragon Ship</td>
    <td>fast</td>
</tr>
<tr>
    <td>Ferry</td>
    <td>slow</td>
</tr>
```

6) Save the code, refresh the web page
You'll see the words in a table, like Figure 39.

Figure 39: a table

2. Adding colours and borders

a. colour the whole table and its borders

Let's colour in the table by using the bgcolor parameter in the table.

1) We can make the whole table yellow by typing this:

```
<table bgcolor="yellow">
     <tr>
          <td>Dragon Ship</td>
```

2) Save the code, go to the web page and refresh it
   The table will be coloured yellow, like Figure 40.

THE NET'S FIRST WORD
The first word sent across the Internet was "Lo" on 26th October 1969. It was actually meant to be "Logon"... but the computers crashed!!

Figure 40: a yellow table

This doesn't look much like a table yet - just words on a yellow background. So, let's put squares round each cell by using border.

3) Type this next to bgcolor="yellow":

```
<table bgcolor="yellow" border="1" bordercolor="black">
     <tr>
```

4) Save the code, and refresh the web page
   The table has a thin black border, like Figure 41.

- border="1" puts in a thin border.
  Try border="5" for a thicker border.
  border="0" will remove the border again.

- *bordercolor="black" colours the border.*
  Try other colours, too!

Figure 41: a black border

Next, more colouring!

b. colour a whole row (using <tr> and bgcolor)

Now let's colour in a whole row.

1) Add a new row above the first one:

```
<table bgcolor="yellow" border="1" bordercolor="black">
    <tr>
        <td>Ship</td>
        <td>Speed</td>
    </tr>
    <tr>
        <td>Dragon Ship</td>
```

2) Now, type bgcolor="red" in the top <tr> tag like this:

```
<table bgcolor="yellow" border="1" bordercolor="black">
    <tr bgcolor="red">
```

3) Save the code, go to the web page and refresh it

The top row of the table will be coloured red, like Figure 42.

TWELVE OR DOZEN?
Strangely, some tags do exactly the same thing (just like "dozen" and "twelve" both mean 12).
Here are three examples:
<i> = <em>
<u> = <ins>
<b> = <strong>
Experts prefer the tags on the right.

12

Figure 42: a row coloured red

c. colour one cell (using <td> and bgcolor)

Now, let's colour in a single cell.
We'll add a new top row and colour one cell white.

1) Type this in under the <table> tag and above the first <tr> tag:

```
<table bgcolor="yellow" border="1" bordercolor="black">
    <tr>
        <td>Our Ships</td>
        <td></td>
    </tr>
    <tr bgcolor="red">
        <td>Ship</td>
```

2) Let's colour the first cell (with "Our Ships" in it) white. Type in this:

```
<tr>
     <td bgcolor="white">Our Ships</td>
     <td></td>
</tr>
```

3) Save the code and refresh the page
The table will now look like Figure 43. It has one white cell.

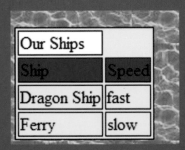

TOP WEB COUNTRIES
The country with the most Internet users is China with 404 million. But this is only 1 in every 3 Chinese.

Figure 43: one cell coloured

3. Stetching cells

a. Stretching a cell across a row (with colspan)

Our table looks odd (again!). It would be better if the whole top row was coloured white with "Our Ships" written in it.
Let's stretch the "Our Ships" cell to cover the top row.

1) Get rid of the <td></td> line under the "Our Ships" cell

```
<tr>
     <td bgcolor="white">Our Ships</td>
</tr>
```

the bottom <td></td> line in this row is gone!

2) Type this in the "Our Ships" cell:

```
<td bgcolor="white" colspan="2">Our Ships</td>
```

3) Save the code, go to the web page and refresh it
The "Our Ships" cell will cover the top row of the table, like Figure 44.

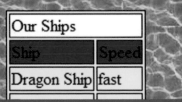

Figure 44: a cell stretched

- *We put colspan = "2" because there are 2 columns in our table.*
- *The table also has 4 rows (like Table 4) .*

WANTED - CONFICKER VIRUS.
Microsoft is offering a
$250, 000 reward to anyone who
can tell police where the people
who made the Conficker virus are.
The virus is really nasty code that
has attacked computers in over
200 countries.

	column 1	column 2
row 1	Our Ships	
row 2	Ship	Speed
row 3	Dragon Ship	fast
row 4	Ferry	slow

Table 4: Ships table

Next we'll see how to make a cell stretch across rows.

b. Stretching a cell across a column (with rowspan)

Let's add another column to our table.
Then, we'll make a cell cover the whole column!

1) Add a cell at the end of the first row by typing <td></td> before the </tr>:

```
<tr>
     <td bgcolor="white" colspan="2">Our Ships</td>
     <td></td>
</tr>
```

2) Make the cell cover the whole column by using rowspan:

```
<tr>
     <td bgcolor="white" colspan="2">Our Ships</td>
     <td rowspan="4"></td>
</tr>
```

The column has 4 rows in it, so we made rowspan="4".
Our table now has 3 columns - like this:

	column 1	column 2	column 3
row 1	Our Ships		
row 2	Ship	Speed	
row 3	Dragon Ship	fast	
row 4	Ferry	slow	

Table 5: Ships table with a new column

3) Add something into the cell.

We're going to add a new picture (see page 21 to do this):
- *we got our picture from the Internet,*
- *and saved it as Man.png in the "images" folder.*

4) Next, add the picture to the page:

```
<tr>
      <td bgcolor="white" colspan="2">Our Ships</td>
      <td rowspan="4"><img src="images/Man.png" /></td>
</tr>
```

5) Save the code and refresh the page

The table will now look like Figure 45.

IDEA
You can change any page on the Internet by doing this:
1. Open the page in Internet Explorer
2. Type this in the address bar:
javascript:document.body.contentEditable='true'; document.designMode='on'; void 0
3. Press Enter
4. Now click on text in the page and change it!!

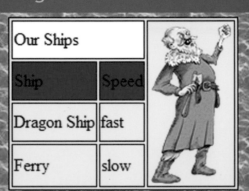

Figure 45: a cell stretched into a column

NOTE
You may need to make the picture bigger or smaller. See page 24 on how to do this.

Finally, let's put the title and the table in the middle of the page.

6) Add this to the code in the <h1> tag and above the <table> tag

```
<h1 align="center">Ships</h1>
<div align="center">
      <table bgcolor="yellow" border="1" bordercolor="black">
```

- *The <div> tags are just like <p> tags - they make paragraphs.*
- *The align="center" puts things in the middle.*

7) Add this to the code below the table

```
      </table>
   </div>
</body>
```

8) Save the code and refresh the page

The table will be in the middle, like Figure 46.

Figure 46: centred table

C. MOVING PICTURES WITH marquee

- we'll fill the Ships page with two pictures of the Viking ship
- and make them move using the marquee tag!!

<marquee> tags make things placed in them move.

1) Type this after the closing </div> tag:

```
</div>
<marquee behavior="scroll" direction="left" scrollamount="1">
    <img src="images/vikship.gif" alt="ship1" /><br />
</marquee>
</body>
```

2) Save the page and refresh it

You can see a ship moving across the page.

Figure 47: moving ship

CODE
The <marquee> tags go round the picture <img /> and <br /> tags.

- behavior="scroll" moves the picture across the screen
- direction="left" moves it from right to left
- scrollamount="1" makes it go slowly

3) Now add a second ship under the first by typing this:

```
</marquee>
<marquee behavior="scroll" direction="left" scrollamount="5">
    <img src="images/vikship.gif" alt="ship2" /><br />
</marquee>
</body>
```

4) Save the page and refresh it

You can see two ships racing each other!

IDEA
To move pictures in different directions, change "left" for one of the following:
"right" to go right
"up" to go up
"down" to go down

CODE
The second ship moves faster than the first because its scrollamount is a higher number (="5")

See how quickly you can make it go by increasing the scrollamount number!

Figure 48: racing ships

CODE

ships.html

```html
<html>
<head><title>Ships</title></head>
<body background="images/IrishSea3.jpg">
    <ul>
        <li>Home</li>
        <li>Ships</li>
        <li>Visiting Ireland</a></li>
        <li>Going berserk</li>
    </ul>
    <h1 align="center">Ships</h1>
    <div align="center">
    <table bgcolor="yellow" border="1" bordercolor="black">
        <tr>
            <td colspan="2" bgcolor="white"
                align="center">Our Ships</td>
            <td rowspan="4"><img src="images/Man.png"></td>
        </tr>
        <tr bgcolor="red">
            <td>Ship</td>
            <td>Speed</td>
        </tr>
        <tr>
            <td>Dragon Ship</td>
            <td>fast</td>
        </tr>
        <tr>
            <td>Ferry</td>
            <td>slow</td>
        </tr>
    </table>
    </div>
<marquee behavior="scroll" direction="left" scrollamount="1">
    <img src="images/vikship.gif" alt="ship1" /><br />
</marquee>
<marquee behavior="scroll" direction="left" scrollamount="5">
    <img src="images/vikship.gif" alt="ship2" /><br />
</marquee>
</body>
</html>
```

Figure 49: Chapter 4 code

Next, sound and video

Chapter 5 – Sound and Video

In this chapter, we'll add some effects to the page which will make you look like a real web genius.

this green part is a navigation bar with all the links in it

a gallery of pictures

this video plays when the page appears

this sound plays when the page appears

the ships move across the screen

FATHER OF CSS
The inventor of CSS is Håkon Lie from Norway. He loves Lego and snowboards and his friends call him "Howcome".

Figure 50: Chapter 5 pages

You don't need to do any of the things in this chapter …
but they'll make the site look very good.

A. MAKING NAVIGATION BARS

Navigation bars contain links to other pages in the website, all in one place on the page - like Table 6.

Let's create another web page and use a table to make a navigation bar.

Our page will have a table that covers the whole page like this:

	column 1	column 2
row 1	Links go here	everything else goes here

Table 6: a navigation bar table

1. Divide the page in two with table and td

1) Follow sections A.2 and 3 on pages 3 and 4 to create a new page:

    a. Call the page "berserk.html"
    b. Open up the code in the page (as described on page 6)

2) Between the <title> tags, type "Go Berserk":

```
<title>Go Berserk</title>
```

3) In the <body> tag, make a table with one row:

```
<body>
    <table>
        <tr>
        </tr>
    </table>
</body>
```

4) Add two cells (and writing) in the table using <td></td>:

```
<tr>
    <td>Home</td>
    <td><h1>Go berserk!!</h1></td>
</tr>
```

The first cell will be a navigation bar. The second is the rest of the page.

5) Make the first cell palegreen

```
<tr>
      <td bgcolor="palegreen">Home</td>
```

6) Make the whole table lightblue with no border (border="0")

```
<body>
      <table bgcolor="lightblue" border="0">
```

7) Next, make the table cover the whole page by using height="100%" and width="100%":

```
<table bgcolor="lightblue" border="0" width="100%" height="100%">
```

8) Save the code and open up the page in a browser
   You'll see this:

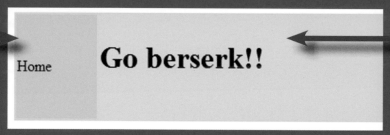

Figure 51: Go Berserk page

2. Put the writing at the top with valign

The writing is in the middle of the page. Let's put it at the top.

1) Type this into the <tr> table row tag:

```
<tr valign="top">
      <td bgcolor="palegreen">Home</td>
```

2) Now let's add the links in the first cell. Type this in:

```
<tr valign="top">
      <td bgcolor="palegreen">
            <a href="index.html">Home</a><br />
            <a href="ships.html">Ships</a><br />
            <a href="http://www.discoverireland.com">
            Visiting Ireland</a><br />
            <a href="berserk.html">Going Berserk</a>
      </td>
```

3) Save the code and refresh the web page

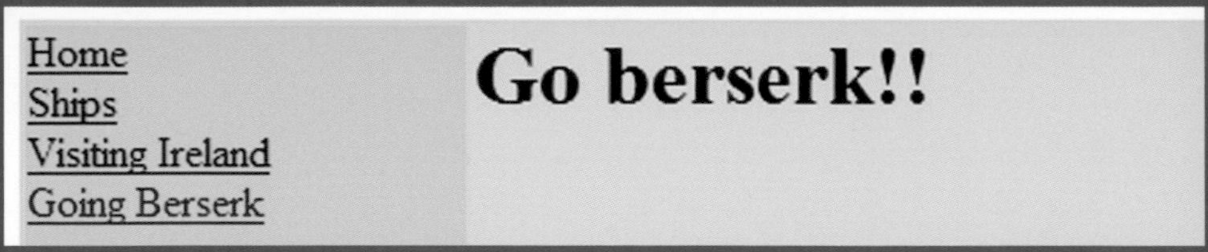

Figure 52: Writing at the top of the page with valign="top"

The last thing we need to do is make the left cell a fixed size.
* *If you make the browser bigger, the left cell gets bigger too.*
* *But we want the left cell to stay a fixed size.*

4) type this into the first <td> tag:

```
<tr valign="top">
      <td bgcolor="palegreen" width="150px">
```

The "150px" makes the cell 150 pixels wide.
* *Pixels are what computers use to measure size (it doesn't understand about centimetres).*
* *A page is 1000 pixels wide and 750 pixels high.*

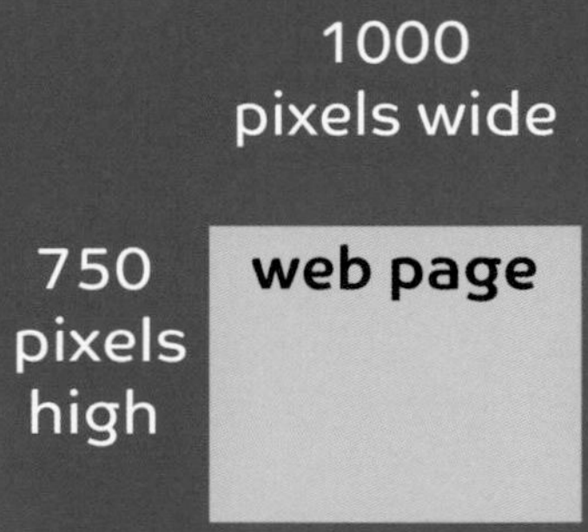

5) Save the code and refresh the web page

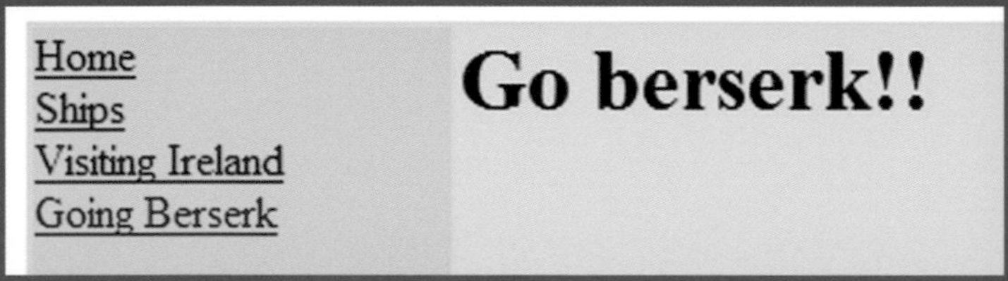

1000
pixels wide

750
pixels
high

web page

Table 7: page

Figure 53: navigation bar with a fixed width

Here's all the table code:

```
<table bgcolor="lightblue" border="0"
     width="100%" height="100%">
     <tr valign="top">
          <td bgcolor="palegreen" width="150px">
               <a href="index.html">Home</a><br />
               <a href="ships.html">Ships</a><br />
               <a href="http://www.discoverireland.com">
                    Visiting Ireland</a><br />
               <a href="berserk.html">Going berserk</a>
          </td>
          <td>
               <h1>Go berserk!!</h1>
          </td>
     </tr>
</table>
```

Next, colouring table borders

3. Making all the pages link together

We've put links to index and ships on the Berserk page. Now we need to make sure the Ships and Index pages have all the right links too.

1) Open up the index.html code and type this around "Going Berserk"

```
<a href="berserk.html">Going berserk</a><br />
```

2) Save the code and refresh the web page
   You will see the new links to the Berserk page.

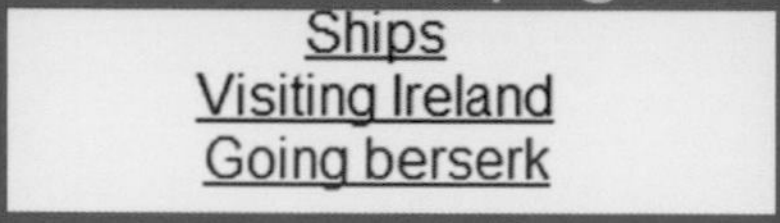

Ships
Visiting Ireland
Going berserk

Figure 54: links on the index.html page

3) Open the code for the ships.html page and add links to the <ul> list:

```
<ul>
    <li><a href="index.html">Home</a></li>
    <li><a href="ships.html">Ships</a></li>
    <li><a href="http://www.discoverireland.com">
        Visiting Ireland</a>
    </li>
    <li><a href="berserk.html">Going berserk</a></li>
</ul>
```

4) Save the code and refresh the page
   The links will appear in the list.

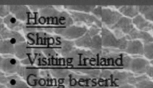

- Home
- Ships
- Visiting Ireland
- Going berserk

Figure 55: links on the Ships page

The links are difficult to read against the blue,
so let's change the background and make the bullet points disappear!

5) Open the code and type this in the first <ul> tag

```
<body background="images/IrishSea3.jpg">
    <ul style="background:palegreen;list-style-type:none;">
```

6) Save the code and refresh the page
   The background will go green!

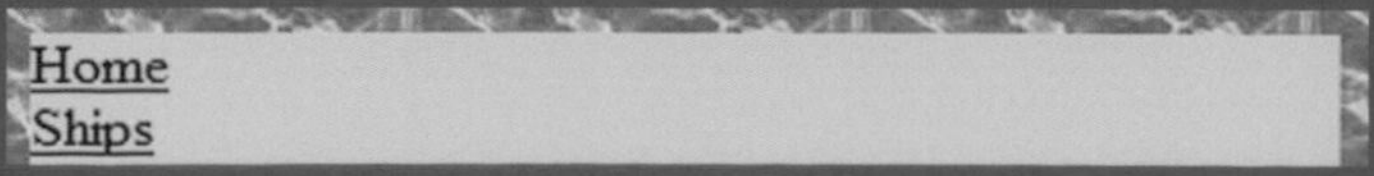

Home
Ships

Figure 56: green background for links

> this is CSS code -
> you can try more
> of it in the
> Appendix

B. TABLE STYLES

Now we're going to make the table on the ships page look better.

1. Centre Writing in Cells

1) Open the Ships code page and type this in the first table row tag `<tr>`

```
<table bgcolor="yellow" border="1" bordercolor="black">
    <tr align="center">
```

2) Save the code and refresh the Ships web page
The "Our Ships" is in the middle!

2. Changing table borders

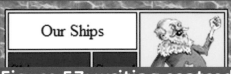

Figure 57: writing centred

If you look closely at the table, it has two borders - one round the table and another round each cell (see Figure 58 and the close-up, Figure 58a) Let's make just one border!

Border round the table

Border round each cell

Figure 58a: table close up

Figure 58: Ships table with blue borders

3) Open up the Ships code and add this into the `<table>` code:

```
<table bgcolor="yellow" border="1" bordercolor="black"
cellspacing="0">
```

- *The **cellspacing** tells the page how much space there is between cells.*

*We've set **cellspacing="0"**, so there is no space.*
This makes the border round each cell disappear!

IDEA
See what happens when you set cellspacing="10"!

4) Save the code and refresh the page

Figure 59: Ships table with a single border

Next, a picture gallery

C. MAKING A PICTURE GALLERY

Lots of websites have pages of pictures. Sometimes these are called picture galleries. Let's put pictures on the berserk page and a table to hold them.

1) Open the berserk.html code and type this in under the heading

```
<h1>Go berserk!!</h1>
<table border="1" bordercolor="black">
    <tr>
        <td></td>
        <td></td>
        <td></td>
    </tr>
    <tr>
        <td></td>
        <td></td>
        <td></td>
    </tr>
</table>
</td>
```

This will make a new table (like Table 5) with:
- *two rows and*
- *three cells in each row.*

Table 8: table

2) Next, go to the Internet and find three pictures you like. Then save them to the images folder.
We have saved these pictures: Man.png, vikship.gif, Us.png.

3) Put the pictures into the cells in the top row by typing this:

```
<table>
    <tr>
        <td><img src="images/Us.png" width="150px"></td>
        <td><img src="images/Man.png" width="150px"></td>
        <td><img src="images/vikship.gif" width="150px"></td>
    </tr>
```

The width="150px" makes sure each picture is only 150 pixels wide.
This means they will all fit in the table.

4) Save the code and refresh the page
The pictures will be side by side.

Figure 60: a picture gallery

D. ADDING SOUND AND VIDEO

1. Adding Video with embed

You can add video and sound to the web page using the <embed> tags.

a. Creating folders for video

We need a new folder called "video" next to the web page.

1) Go to the folder which contains the web page

2) Right-click in a space and choose "New" then "Folder"
   A new folder will be created.

3) Name the folder "video"

INTERNET VIDEOS
The most popular Internet video of all time is the Star Wars kid playing with a lightsabre.

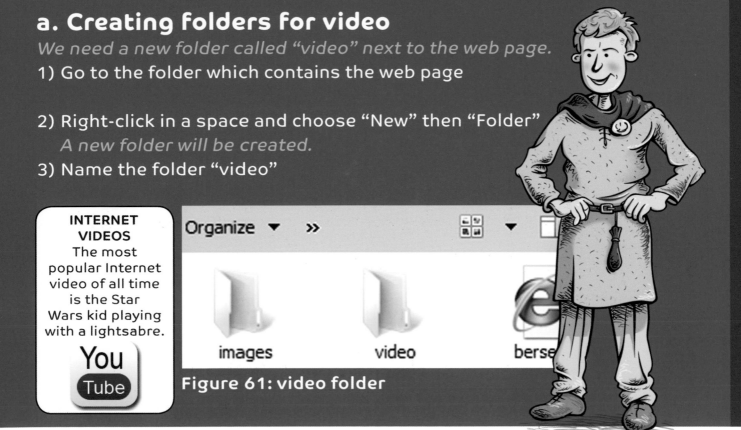

Figure 61: video folder

b. Download video files

Here is a table which lists the most common video formats.
It lists their file extensions (the 3 letter code which follows the name of the file) and some comments to help you decide which to use.

Format	File Extension	Good?	Comments
AVI (Audio Video Interleave)	.avi e.g. video.avi	✓	popular but may not work on non-Windows computers, and has a very large file size
MPEG (Moving Pictures Expert Group)	.mpg or .mpeg e.g. video.mpg	✓✓✓	most popular video format, but has a very large file size
Quick Time	.mov e.g. video.mov	✗	needs a download for it to work on Windows computers
Flash	.swf e.g. video.swf	✓✓	small file size but does not work on Macintosh computers (e.g. iPad)

Table 9: video file formats

> **NOTE**
> It's better to have a small file size (less than 1MB) so that the page will show up quickly.

1) Go onto the Internet and search for a video you like

2) Right-click on the video and choose "Save As"

3) Browse to the "video" folder you created and choose "Save"
The video will be saved to the "video" folder.
We have saved a video called video.swf into the "video" folder.

c. Add video to the page

Let's add a video to the Berserk page gallery table.

1) Open the berserk.html code
First, let's stretch one cell in the bottom row to cover the whole row.
2) Remove two <td></td> tags from the bottom row and type

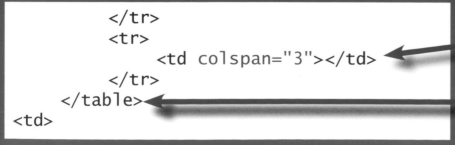

```
        </tr>
        <tr>
            <td colspan="3"></td>
        </tr>
    </table>
<td>
```

the bottom two <td></td> lines in this row are gone!

this is the end of the table that contains the pictures

3) Now add this into the cell on the bottom row

```
    <tr>
        <td colspan="3">
            <embed src="video/video.swf" autostart="true"
                loop="false" width="480px" height="640px">
            </embed>
        </td>
    </tr>
</table>
```

The *<embed>* tag is like a *<img />* tag, it has:
* *src*, which says where to find the video file
* *width* and *height*, which say how big the video will be (in pixels).

But it also has two new parameters:
* *loop="false"* tells the page to play the video once
* *autostart="true"* starts the video as soon as the page appears.
And it needs a closing tag, *</embed>*!

4) Save the code and refresh the web page
The video you have chosen will appear in the table.
It will play as soon as the web page appears.

Figure 62: video on the page

2. Adding sounds with embed

We've added video to the page. Now let's add sounds using <embed> tags.

a. Download sound files

Repeat the steps in "b. Download video files" on page 48, except:
- look for a sound you like,
- and create a folder called "sounds" to put it in.
  We have saved a sound called sound.wav into the "sounds" folder.

Here is a table which lists the most common sound formats.

Format	File Extension	Good?	Comments
MIDI (Musical Instrument Digital Interface)	.mid or .midi e.g. sound.mid	✓	popular but may not work on non-very small, but only records notes (like A#), not sounds (like singing)
Wave	.wav e.g. sound.wav	✓✓✓	most popular sound format, but can't be used in Chrome browser
MPEG (Moving Pictures Experts Group)	.mp3 or .mpga e.g. sound.mp3	✗	very popular for recorded music and high quality

Table 10: sound file formats

b. Add sounds to the page
Let's add the sound to the Berserk page.

1) Open the berserk.html code page

2) After the last </embed> tag, add this:

> **18 HOURS PER WEEK?**
> A recent survey says the average person is on the Internet 13 hours every week (twice as long as 5 years ago). But if you're between 25 and 50, you surf 18 hours a week..
>
>

```
<td colspan="3">
    <embed src="video/video.swf" autostart="true"
        loop="false" width="480px" height="640px">
    </embed><br />
    <embed src="sounds/sound.wav" autostart="true"
        loop="false" width="1px" height="1px">
    </embed>
</td>
```

The new `<embed>` code is nearly the same as the old one.
- *src* says where to find the sound file
- *autostart="true"* plays the sound as soon as the page appears
- *loop="false"* tells the page to play the sound once

- *width* and *height* say how big the sound will be on the page (in pixels).

But, since we don't want to see the sound (just hear it!)
- *width* and *height* are very very small, just 1 pixel big (="1px").

3) Save the code and refresh the web page
   The sound will automatically be played as soon as the page appears.

Figure 63: video and sound playing on the page

FATHERS OF THE GALACTIC WIDE WEB
The Internet has lots of fathers: in 1962 J.C.R Licklider dreamt of a "Galactic Network" of computers. In 1974 Nam June Paik imagined a "super highway" of computers carrying information between cities.

Next, all the code put together 51

CODE

files

Here is a list of all the files we have made:

- index.html
- ships.html
- berserk.html

In the "images" folder:
- vikship.gif
- Man.png
- picture.png
- Us.png

In the "sounds" folder:
- sound.wav

In the "video" folder:
- video.swf

Here is the finished code for all the pages:

MYSTERY MEAT NAVIGATION
If you find a web page with links which don't tell you where they go to, experts call them "Mystery Meat Navigation". This is because Americans call meals with unidentifiable meat 'mystery meat'.

HOW WORLD WIDE WEB?
Worldwide, 1 in 4 people are online (1.8 billion).. but not all at once.

index.html

```html
<html>
    <head><title>Home Page</title></head>
    <body font-family="Arial, Serif" bgcolor="yellow"
        text="blue">
        <h1 align="center">Our Home Page.</h1>
        <p align="center">
            <font color="red" size="3" face="Jokerman">
                Hello.</font><br />
                <u><b><i>This site is all about our favourite
                things</i></b></u>
        </p>
    <p align="center">here is a list of things we like:<br />
        <a href="ships.html">Ships</a><!--cool!--><br />
        <a href="http://www.discoverireland.com">
            Visiting Ireland</a><br />
        <a href="berserk.html">Going berserk</a><br />
        </p>
```

```
          <p><img src="images/vikship.gif" alt="ship"
                   height="40%" width="40%" />
               <img src="images/picture.gif" alt="Us"
                   height="50%" width="50%" /></p>
      </body>
</html>
```

berserk.html

```
<html>
    <head>
        <title>Go Berserk</title>
    </head>
    <body>
        <table bgcolor="lightblue" border="0"
            width="100%"  height="100%">
            <tr valign="top">
                <td width="150px" bgcolor="palegreen">
                    <a href="index.html">Home</a><br />
                    <a href="ships.html">Ships</a><br />
                <a href="http://www.discoverireland.com">
                    Visiting Ireland</a><br />
                    <a href="berserk.html">
                        Going Berserk</a>
                </td>
                <td valign="top">
                    <h1>Go berserk!!</h1>
                    <table border="1" bordercolor="black">
                        <tr>
                            <td>
                            <img src="images/Us.png"
                                    width="150px">
                            </td>
                            <td>
                            <img src="images/Man.png"
                                    width="150px">
                            </td>
                            <td>
                            <img src="images/vikship.gif"
                                    width="150px">
                            </td>
                        </tr>
```

YOUNGEST
MICROSOFT EXPERT
8 year old Marko Calasan
from Macedonia is the
youngest person to pass
a Microsoft exam.
He is a Microsoft
Certified IT Professional.

Next, more code put together   53

```
                    <tr>
                        <td colspan="3">
                            <embed src="video/video.swf" autostart="true"
                                loop="false" width="480px" height="640px">
                            </embed><br />
                            <embed src="sounds/sound.wav" autostart="true"
                                loop="false" width="1px" height="1px">
                            </embed>
                        </td>
                    </tr>
                </table>
            </body>
        </html>
```

ships.html

```
<html>
    <head>
        <title>Ships</title>
    </head>
    <body background="images/IrishSea3.jpg" >
        <ul style="background:palegreen; list-style-type:none;">
            <li><a href="index.html">Home</a></li>
            <li><a href="ships.html">Ships</a></li>
            <li><a href="http://www.discoverireland.com">
                Visiting Ireland</a></li>
            <li><a href="berserk.html">Going berserk</a></li>
        </ul>
        <h1 align="center">Ships</h1>
        <div align="center">
        <table bgcolor="yellow" border="1" bordercolor="black"
            cellspacing="0">
            <tr>
                <td colspan="2" bgcolor="white">Our Ships</td>
                <td rowspan="4">
                    <img src="images/Man.png" width="100px" />
                </td>
            </tr>
            <tr bgcolor="red">
                <td>Ship</td>
                <td>Speed</td>
            </tr>
```

```
                    <tr>
                        <td>Dragon Ship</td>
                        <td>fast</td>
                    </tr>
                    <tr>
                        <td>Ferry</td>
                        <td>slow</td>
                    </tr>
                </table>
                </div>
<marquee behavior="scroll" direction="left"
scrollamount="1">
        <img src="images/vikship.gif" alt="ship1" />
        <br />
</marquee>
<marquee behavior="scroll" direction="left"
scrollamount="5">
        <img src="images/vikship.gif" alt="ship2" />
        <br />
</marquee>
</body></html>
```

Figure 64: Chapter 5 code

We're all web geniuses!!

Next, put the website online

You've made your web site on your computer. To put it on the Internet, you need to copy the files to a computer on the Internet, called a "web host".
- *you don't need to put your site on the Internet unless you want everyone, anywhere to see it.*

tricky and not really necessary

A. GET WEB SPACE ON A WEB HOST

1) Search for "free web host" in a search engine (or try the lists at
http://www.free-webhosts.com/webhosting-01.php)

What you want	What this means
100 MB of space or more	100 MB is enough space for a simple website
no ads from other people	you don't want people's adverts on your site
no banners	a banner is an advert across the top of the page
allows subdomains	You choose a name for your web site. Some web hosts allow you to choose a Subdomain where your chosen name is followed by the web host's name – like www.mysite.freewebserver.com.
upload using FTP	this allows you to use FileZilla described below

Table 11: what you want from a web host

WEB WORDS
FTP stands for File Transfer Protocol. It allows you to put your files onto the Internet

2) Go to the web host's Internet address and register (e.g.
http://webhosting-for-free.com/register/new_reg.php)

NOTE
Some web hosts allow you to choose a domain. This means the web host's name does not appear in your website's name, like www.mysite.com

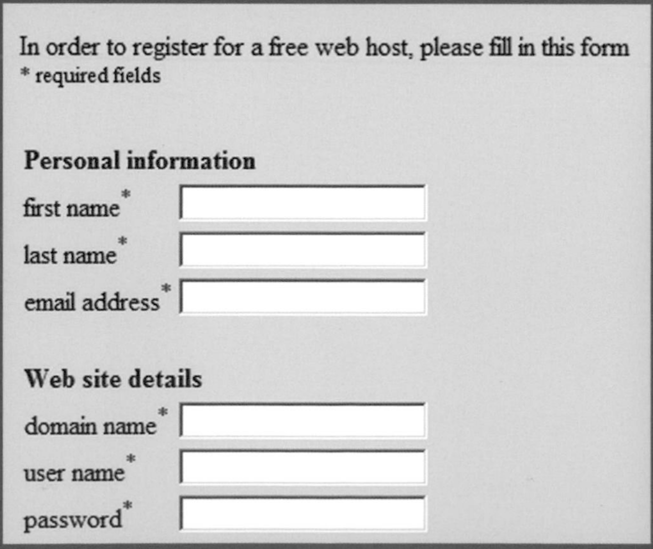

In order to register for a free web host, please fill in this form
* required fields

Personal information

first name*

last name*

email address*

Web site details

domain name*

user name*

password*

Figure 65: web host registration

You will need to give:
- your name and email address
- a name for your website
  (sometimes called "domain" or "subdomain")
- a user name and a password.

You will use these to get into your website.

3) You may be asked to:
   a. Enter a code shown on the registration page

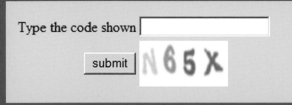

Figure 66: registration page asking for a code

b. *(if the web host emails you a link to make your account work)*
   Click on the link the web host emails to you

To activate your Account, you should click on link below:

http://webhosting-for-free.com/register/new_reg.php?auth=TVRNeU99EY3

Figure 67: email from web host

- *It may take a day for the web host to make your web space.*
- *You will also get an email address for the website.*

> my email address is
> 'snorri@snorri.heliohost.org'

Your website's name will be 'www.' then the name you choose, then another '.' then the web host name *e.g.* www.snorri.heliohost.org.

Here are my website details:
- *the web host name is '**heliohost.org**'*
- *the website name is '**snorri**' (it's a famous Viking name)*
- *the user name is also '**snorri**'*
- *I won't tell you my password!*

My website will be called 'www.snorri.heliohost.org'.

WORST PASSWORDS
Make sure you choose a password that can't be guessed.

Here are some of the most common passwords:
michael (14), football (15) jennifer (26), batman (31), trustno1 (32), tigger (34), love (37), superman (47).

1 in 10 Internet users uses a password in the top 500.

B. INSTALL FILEZILLA

1) Go to filezilla-project.org/download.php?type=client

2) Download the version of FileZilla for your computer (e.g. Windows, Mac)

3) Double-click on the file you have downloaded to install FileZilla
   The Set up window will appear.

Figure 68: FileZilla setup

> **WEB WORDS**
> Here is a web address:
> www.books.google.com
> Its parts are split up by dots:
> - <u>com</u> means it's a (big) company
> - <u>google</u> is the domain – the company's name
> - <u>books</u> is a subdomain – a part of the company
> - <u>www</u> is the part of books on the <u>W</u>orld <u>W</u>ide <u>W</u>eb – it's website

a. Click on "I Agree" (to agree to the license)
b. Click on "Yes" to install FileZilla on your computer
c. Click "Next" to install the program's parts
d. Click "Next" to install Filezilla in a Filezilla folder
e. Click "Install"
   The program will install.
f. Click "Finish" to launch Filezilla
   FileZilla's window will appear.

if you get really stuck click on "Help"

this is where the files on your computer will appear

click on ✗ to close FileZilla

drag files from the left to the right to put them on the web host

this is where the web host's files appear

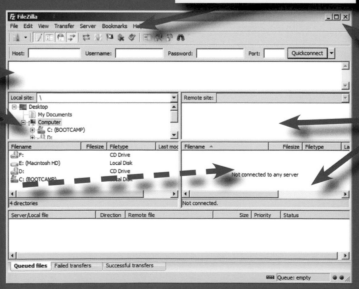

Figure 69: FileZilla window

C. ADD PAGES TO A WEB HOST ⓘ ✕

1) In the top part of the window, type:
   a. your web site name (in the "Host:" box)
      (you'll probably need to put 'ftp.' in front - see my website's details below for an example)
   b. your user name (in the "Username:" box)
   c. your password (in the "Password:" box)
   leave the "Port:" box empty!

"Quickconnect" button

"Host:" box   "Username:" box   "Password:" box   "Port:" box

Host: ftp.snorri.heliohost.o Username: snorri Password: •••••••• Port: [   ] Quickconnect ▼

Figure 70: typing in web host details

Here are my website's details:
- *my web site is 'snorri.heliohost.org' (but we need to put ftp. in front), so my **Host:** is '**ftp.snorri.heliohost.org**'*
- *my **Username:** is '**snorri**'*
- *my **Password:** is still secret!*

> **NOTE**
> 1. Make sure you type in the user name and password exactly, including capitals. Since 'snorri' is my user name, FileZilla won't accept 'Snorri'.
> 2. You don't need to fill in the 'Port' (but it's usually 21)

2) Click "Quickconnect".
   The web site's folders will appear in the web site side of the window.

3) Double-click on a folder called "www" to open up the web pages folder (you might have to use the scroll bar to find it)

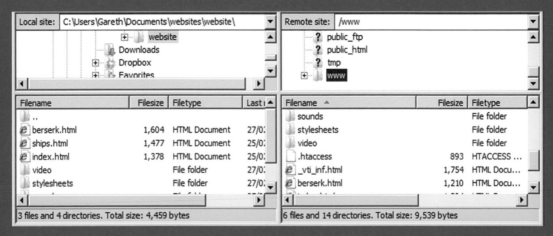

Figure 71: "www" folder on the web host

4) In the left hand side, find the folder on your computer where your web site is
(Double-click on the folders you put the site in until you find it)

Filezilla gives you (sometimes helpful) messages here

Double-click on these folders until you find the web site folder on your computer

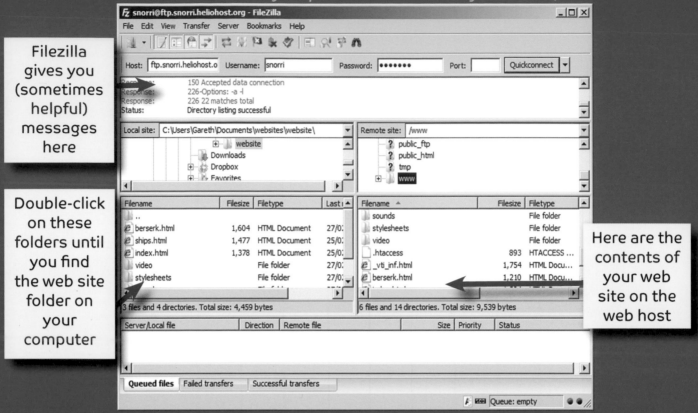

Here are the contents of your web site on the web host

Figure 72: the web site on your computer

5) Click on each file and folder you want to put onto the web host:
   a. Hold the left mouse down
   b. Drag the file or folder to the "www" folder
   c. Let go of the left mouse to drop the file or folder in "www"

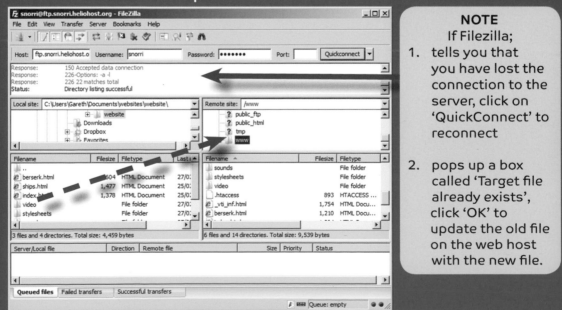

NOTE
If Filezilla;
1. tells you that you have lost the connection to the server, click on 'QuickConnect' to reconnect

2. pops up a box called 'Target file already exists', click 'OK' to update the old file on the web host with the new file.

Figure 73: copying "video" folder to the "www" folder

The files and folders will be copied across.
If you copy a folder, all the files in the folder will be copied too!

6) Repeat step 5 until you have copied all the files and folders in your web site to the web host

7) Click on the x in the top right of the FileZilla window to close it

8) Open up a browser window and type in the name of your website to see the changes

Your web site's name will be like this: www.mysite.webhost.com/index.html
(replace mysite with the name you chose for your site, and webhost.com with your web host's name)

So, my site is called www.snorri.heliohost.org/index.html.

MORE WEB WORDS
'Web hosts' can also be called 'web servers'. They are huge computers which put people's web sites on the Internet.

'snorri' is the name I chose for my site

'heliohost.org' is the name of my web host

'index.html' is the first page on the web site

IDEA
To allow Google to look for your site, go to www.google.com/addurl and add your web site's address, e.g. http://www.snorri.heliohost.org

World Wide Web, here we come!!

Next, some more useful things

A. COLOUR NAMES

This section lists all the colours by name. In brackets after the name it also lists the colours by the code the computer recognizes (hex code).

- This code is called "hex code" because instead of using the ten numbers from 0 to 9 (decimal code), it uses 16 numbers (hexadecimal code) – the numbers from 0 to 9, and the letters from A to F (for 10 to 15).
- A hash (#) is written before the code, so you know it's hexadecimal. You can use this code instead of the colour name if you really want to.

Here are some examples of hex numbers:

Hex	Decimal	Hex	Decimal	Hex	Decimal
0	0	0DD	221	F00D	61453
2	2	BABE	47806	BE	190
A	10	C0FFEE	13648430	FF	255
F	16	BAD	2989	80	128

Table 12: some hex numbers

Here are the 16 basic colours:

black #000000	navy #000080	blue #0000FF	green #008000	teal #008080	lime #00FF00	aqua #00FFFF	maroon #800000
purple #800080	olive #808000	gray #808080	silver #C0C0C0	red #FF0000	fuschia #FF00FF	yellow #FFFF00	white #FFFFFF

Table 13: the 16 basic colours with their hex codes

Here are the 124 additional colours:
(see www.go-berserk.com/htmlcolours.html for the colours)

AliceBlue (#F0F8FF)
AntiqueWhite (#FAEBD7)
Aqua (#00FFFF)
Aquamarine (#7FFFD4)
Azure (#F0FFFF)
Beige (#F5F5DC)
Bisque (#FFE4C4)
Black (#000000)
BlanchedAlmond (#FFEBCD)
Blue (#0000FF)
BlueViolet (#8A2BE2)
Brown (#A52A2A)

BurlyWood (#DEB887)
CadetBlue (#5F9EA0)
Chartreuse (#7FFF00)
Chocolate (#D2691E)
Coral (#FF7F50)
CornflowerBlue (#6495ED)
Cornsilk (#FFF8DC)
Crimson (#DC143C)
Cyan (#00FFFF)
DarkBlue (#00008B)
DarkCyan (#008B8B)
DarkGoldenRod (#B8860B)

DarkGray (#A9A9A9)
DarkGreen (#006400)
DarkKhaki (#BDB76B)
AliceBlue (#F0F8FF)
DarkMagenta (#8B008B)
DarkOliveGreen (#556B2F)
Darkorange (#FF8C00)
DarkOrchid (#9932CC)
DarkRed (#8B0000)
DarkSalmon (#E9967A)
DarkSeaGreen (#8FBC8F)
DarkSlateBlue (#483D8B)

DarkSlateGray (#2F4F4F)
DarkTurquoise (#00CED1)
DarkViolet (#9400D3)
DeepPink (#FF1493)
DeepSkyBlue (#00BFFF)
DimGray (#696969)
DodgerBlue (#1E90FF)
FireBrick (#B22222)
FloralWhite (#FFFAF0)
ForestGreen (#228B22)
Fuchsia (#FF00FF)
Gainsboro (#DCDCDC)
GhostWhite (#F8F8FF)
Gold (#FFD700)
GoldenRod (#DAA520)
Gray (#808080)
Green (#008000)
GreenYellow (#ADFF2F)
HoneyDew (#F0FFF0)
HotPink (#FF69B4)
IndianRed (#CD5C5C)
Indigo (#4B0082)
Ivory (#FFFFF0)
Khaki (#F0E68C)
Lavender (#E6E6FA)
LavenderBlush (#FFF0F5)
LawnGreen (#7CFC00)
LemonChiffon (#FFFACD)
LightBlue (#ADD8E6)
LightCoral (#F08080)
LightCyan (#E0FFFF)
LightGoldenRodYellow
(#FAFAD2)
LightGrey (#D3D3D3)
LightGreen (#90EE90)
LightPink (#FFB6C1)
LightSalmon (#FFA07A)
LightSeaGreen (#20B2AA)

LightSkyBlue (#87CEFA)
LightSlateGray (#778899)
LightSteelBlue (#B0C4DE)
LightYellow (#FFFFE0)
Lime (#00FF00)
LimeGreen (#32CD32)
Linen (#FAF0E6)
Magenta (#FF00FF)
Maroon (#800000)
MediumAquaMarine
(#66CDAA)
MediumBlue (#0000CD)
MediumOrchid (#BA55D3)
MediumPurple (#9370D8)
MediumSeaGreen
(#3CB371)
MediumSlateBlue
(#7B68EE)
MediumSpringGreen
(#00FA9A)
MediumTurquoise
(#48D1CC)
MediumVioletRed
(#C71585)
MidnightBlue (#191970)
MintCream (#F5FFFA)
MistyRose (#FFE4E1)
Moccasin (#FFE4B5)
NavajoWhite (#FFDEAD)
Navy (#000080)
OldLace (#FDF5E6)
Olive (#808000)
OliveDrab (#6B8E23)
Orange (#FFA500)
OrangeRed (#FF4500)
Orchid (#DA70D6)
PaleGoldenRod (#EEE8AA)
PaleGreen (#98FB98)

PaleTurquoise (#AFEEEE)
PaleVioletRed (#D87093)
PapayaWhip (#FFEFD5)
PeachPuff (#FFDAB9)
Peru (#CD853F)
Pink (#FFC0CB)
Plum (#DDA0DD)
PowderBlue (#B0E0E6)
Purple (#800080)
Red (#FF0000)
RosyBrown (#BC8F8F)
RoyalBlue (#4169E1)
SaddleBrown (#8B4513)
Salmon (#FA8072)
SandyBrown (#F4A460)
SeaGreen (#2E8B57)
SeaShell (#FFF5EE)
Sienna (#A0522D)
Silver (#C0C0C0)
SkyBlue (#87CEEB)
SlateBlue (#6A5ACD)
SlateGray (#708090)
Snow (#FFFAFA)
SpringGreen (#00FF7F)
SteelBlue (#4682B4)
Tan (#D2B48C)
Teal (#008080)
Thistle (#D8BFD8)
Tomato (#FF6347)
Turquoise (#40E0D0)
Violet (#EE82EE)
Wheat (#F5DEB3)
White (#FFFFFF)
WhiteSmoke (#F5F5F5)
Yellow (#FFFF00)
YellowGreen (#9ACD32)

B. WEB PAGE FONTS

Here are fonts found on most computers - avoid using fonts not on this list.
Arial, **Arial Black**, Book Antiqua, Comic Sans MS, Courier New,
Geneva, Helvetica, **Impact**, Lucida Console, Monaco, Palatino
Linotype, Symbol (Σψμβολ), Tahoma, Times New Roman, Trebuchet MS,
Verdana, Webdings (▶️📷🚲♥️ℹ️●■?)

C. CASCADING STYLE SHEETS (CSS)

This section gives lots of ideas for your site.
You don't need to use any of them, but they'll make your site look great!
Cascading Style Sheets (CSS for short) allow you to do lots of great things
with a web page, like making things change colour.

You can use CSS styles by:
• Creating a style sheet file with lots of styles in it *or*
• Putting a style parameter in a tag or page you want to use a style in.

1. Create the style sheet file

> **NOTE**
> We've actually already
> used CSS!
> Take a look at pages
> 14 and 44 to see
> where.

a. Create a folder and style sheet

1) Create a folder called "stylesheets" (see page 20)

2) Right-click in the folder and select "New" then "Text Document" in the list
   A new text document will appear.

> **HOW BIG IS THE INTERNET?**
> In 1994 there were 624 web sites.
> In 2010 there were 234 million web
> sites with 15 billion web pages.
> That's 3 pages for every human
> being on the planet.

3) Double-click on it to open it up

4) Click on "File" then "Save As"

5) Type in the name you want to call the page in the "File name" box
   We will call ours style.css (make sure you type .css after the name).

6) In the drop-down list next to "Save as type:", select "All files"

7) Click on "Save". *The computer will now save the file as a style sheet.*

b. Create a link to the stylesheet

On every page you want to use the stylesheet, type this at the top:

```
<?xml version="1.0" encoding="UTF-8"?>
<!DOCTYPE html>
<html>
    <head>
        <link rel="stylesheet" href="stylesheets/style.css"
            type="text/css">
```

2. Colour links

On some web pages, links change colour when you click on them or even when you put the mouse over them. Here is how to do it with CSS.

1) Go to the code of the index.html page.

2) Around the `<html>` and `<head>` tags, add in the stylesheet code:

```
<?xml version="1.0" encoding="UTF-8"?>
<!DOCTYPE html>
<html>
    <head>
        <link rel="stylesheet" href="stylesheets/style.css"
            type="text/css">
```

3) Open up the style.css file and type in this:

```
a:link {color: purple;}
```

This code turns any links on your page purple

CSS CODE STYLE
- The CSS changes what happens to links in `<a>` tags, so it starts with 'a'.
- The instructions in brackets {} tells the link how to change.
  - Each instruction ends in a semicolon (';'),
  - Each has a parameter (e.g. color) and a value (e.g. purple).
  - Instead of HTML's '=' CSS uses a colon ':' e.g. color:purple
  - It doesn't use speech marks "..." round the numbers or words

4) Save the style sheet and the index.html code page

5) Go to the web page and refresh it

here is a list of things we like:
Ships
Visiting Ireland
Going berserk

Figure 74: using CSS a:link to turn links purple

In Internet Explorer, you may get this warning. Click on it, it's safe.

 To help protect your security, Internet Explorer has restricted this webpage from running scripts or ActiveX controls that could access...

Figure 75: Internet Explorer warning

Next, glowing writing

You can make other changes to links by typing this after the **a:link** *code in the style sheet.*

```
a:link {color: purple;}
a:visited {color: green;}
a:hover {color: red;}
a:active {color: blue;}
```

CODE

- The a:visited code colours links that have been clicked green.
- The a:hover code colours links red when you hover your mouse over them.
- The a:active code colours links blue when they are clicked.

You need to type all these in this order for them to work.

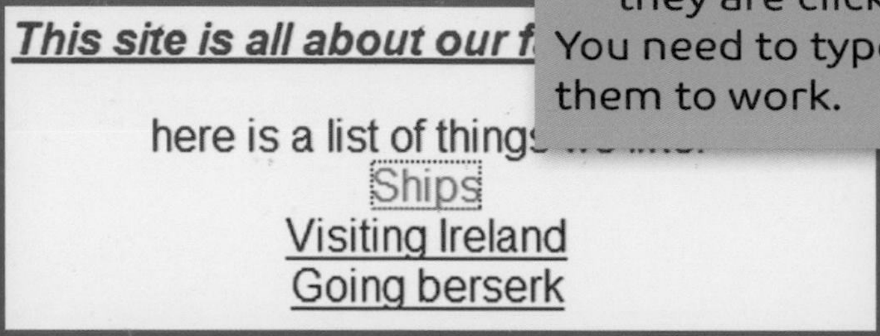

This site is all about our f
here is a list of things
Ships
Visiting Ireland
Going berserk

Figure 76: visited link gone green

INTERNET TIME
Studies show that the average teenager spends 7 ½ hours a day on multimedia (Internet, computer games and mobile phones), but actually does 11 hours worth of watching (because they watch two or more things at once)!!!

3. Hiding Bullet Points with style

On page 44, we coloured the links on ships.html.
Each link used to have bullet points,
then we removed the bullet points and coloured the link green.

BEFORE
Home
Ships
Visiting Ireland
Going berserk
AFTER
Home
Ships
Visiting Ireland
Going berserk

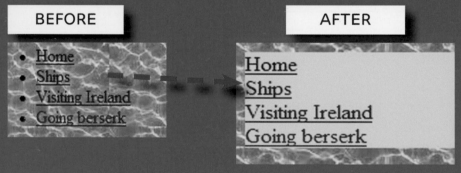

Figure 77: ships list before and after adding style

CODE
The style code only changes this ul tag:

- it removes any numbers or bullets in front of the items in the list (list-style-type: none;)
- and it colours the list palegreen (background: palegreen;)

1) Open the ships.html code
   This is what we put in the **ul** *tag:*

```
<body background="images/IrishSea3.jpg">
    <ul style="background:palegreen;list-style-type:none;">
        <li><a href="index.html">Home</a></li>
```

We only want this list to go green and lose the bullet points (not every list on every page). So,

- *we've put the CSS code only on this page,*
- *and in the* **ul** *tag for the list in a* **style** *attribute.*

D. ADVANCED CSS

The CSS we have looked at so far have only needed a few lines.
These next examples need more lines, because different lines apply to
different browsers. Some are for Internet Explorer, some for Firefox etc.

1. Make text glow ⓘ ✕

This code will make writing glow.

CODE
Type class="glow" in a tag to
make it glow.
- The writing in the tag will be
  white (color:white;)

1) Open the style.css page and add this:

```css
.glow {
    filter: progid:DXImageTransform.Microsoft.glow(Color=red,
        Strength=20);
    text-shadow: 0 0 0.2em red;
    color: white;
}
```

- The filter line works in
  Internet Explorer and the
  text-shadow in other
  browsers.
- Both make the glow red and
  very strong (Strength=20 and
  0.2em)

2) Open the Berserk code and add this:

```html
<?xml version="1.0" encoding="UTF-8"?>
<!DOCTYPE html>
<html>
    <head>
        <link rel="stylesheet" href="stylesheets/style.css"
            type="text/css">
        <title>Go Berserk!!</title>
    </head>
```

3) Open up the Ships code page and add the same lines in

4) Save the Ships code page
   We'll add more effects to it later on!

5) On the Berserk code page type class="glow" in the <h1> tag with "Go
   berserk" in it

```html
<h1 class="glow">Go berserk!!</h1>
```

6) Save the style.css page and the beserk code and refresh the web page
   The text in the tag will now be coloured white with a red glow...

Next, writing with a shadow

Figure 78: text glowing

2. <u>Give text a shadow</u>

This code will give the text a red shadow.

1) Open up style.css and add this at the bottom

```
.redshadow {
    filter: progid:DXImageTransform.Microsoft.Shadow(color=red,
        direction=135);
    text-shadow: 0.1em 0.1em 0.05em purple;
    color:white;
}
```

CODE
This is almost the same as the glow code, except for 2 things:

1. the writing is not blurry (there is no Strength mentioned and the blur is very small: 0.05em)
2. the writing has a slant (direction=135 and 0.1em, 0.1em).

2) Open up the Ships code and add this to the h1 tag

```
<h1 align="center" class="redshadow">Ships</
```

3) Save the style.css page and the ships.html code

4) Go to the ships.html web page and refresh it
   The text will be coloured white with a red shadow. You can change the colours for any named colour.

Figure 79: text with a shadow

Let's do the same for index.html, but we'll give the shadow a blue colour.

5) Open up the style.css code and add this at the bottom:

```
.blueshadow {
    filter: progid:DXImageTransform.Microsoft.Shadow
        (color=purple,direction=135);
    text-shadow: 0.1em 0.1em 0.05em purple;
    color:dodgerblue;
}
```

CODE
This is almost the same as the redshadow code, except:
- the shadow colour is purple
- the writing colour is dodgerblue
- the size is smaller (0.1em)

6) Open up the index.html code page

7) Add class="blueshadow" to <h1>

```
<h1 align="center" class="blueshadow">Our Home Page.</h1>
```

8) Save the style.css page and the index.html code

9) Go to the index.html web page and refresh it to see what happened
The heading will now have a blue shadow.

A LONG WEBSITE NAME
The maximum number of characters you can have in your website name is 63. Google.com has 5 characters. Strangely, there are 63 website names made up of just the letter a, starting with a.com (with 1 "a" character) to "a" followed by 62 more "a"s .com.

Figure 80: Home page with a shadow on the heading

Next, colours merging into eachother

3. Make colours merge together

This code will change one colour at the top of the page gradually into another at the bottom - like mixing colours.

1) Open the index.html code and add this in the body tag:

```
<body class="gradient" style="font-family
```

> **CODE**
> This code
> (style="height: 100%")
> makes the colours
> cover the whole page.

2) Around the <html> and <head> tags, add this:

```
<html style="height: 100%;">
    <head>
        <link rel="stylesheets" href="stylesheets/style.css"
            type="text/css" >
```

3) Open up the style.css code

4) Add this at the end:

> **CODE**
> There are 5 lines of code:

```
.gradient {
    background: -webkit-gradient(linear, left top,
left bottom, from(white), to(lightblue));
    background: -moz-linear-gradient(top, white, lightblue);
    filter: progid:DXImageTransform.Microsoft.
gradient(startColorstr=white, endColorstr=lightblue);
    -ms-filter: "progid:DXImageTransform.Microsoft.
gradient(startColorstr=white, endColorstr=lightblue)";
    height: 100%;
    margin: 0;
}
```

> The colours fill the whole page
> (height: 100%; margin: 0;)
> The other lines colour 4 browsers:
> • Chrome: -webkit-gradient
> • Firefox: –moz-linear-gradient
> • Internet Explorer: old (filter) and
>   new (-ms-filter).
> Each line mentions the start colour
> (white) and the end colour
> (lightblue)

This code will merge colours:
• it starts with **white** at the top,
• and becomes **lightblue** at the end.

We have used white and lightblue.
But you can use any colour.
Just replace our colour names with yours.

5) Save the index.html code and the style.css code

6) Go to the index.html web page and refresh it

Figure 81: colours merging into each other

E. WEB SITE DESCRIPTION

People can search for your website on the Internet using search engines like Google. Some search engines know what your site is about by looking at its description in special `<meta />` tags in the `<head>` tags.

1) Open ships.html and add this under the `<head>`:

```
<head>
        <meta name="description" content="Our Vikings website" />
        <meta name="keywords" content="Vikings Ships Berserk" />
```

2) Save the page
You won't see anything, but Search Engines will.

You can add `<meta />` tags to all pages.

CODE
There are two `<meta />` tags:
- `name="description"` contains a sentence that describes the website (in `content=`).
- `name="keywords"` gives words that best describe the website (in `content=`).

Next, all the code put together   71

CODE

at the top of index.html, ships.html and berserk.html

```
<?xml version="1.0" encoding="UTF-8"?>
<!DOCTYPE html>
<html><head>
    <meta name="description" content="Our Vikings website" />
    <meta name="keywords" content="Vikings Ships Berserk" />
<link rel="stylesheet" href="stylesheets/style.css" type="text/css"
/>
```

style.css

```
.gradient {
    background: -webkit-gradient(linear, left top,
        left bottom, from(white), to(lightblue));
    background: -moz-linear-gradient(top, white, lightblue);
    filter: progid:DXImageTransform.Microsoft.gradient
        (startColorstr=white, endColorstr=lightblue);
    -ms-filter: "progid:DXImageTransform.Microsoft.gradient
        (startColorstr=white, endColorstr=lightblue)";
    height: 100%;
    margin: 0;
}
.blueshadow {
    filter: progid:DXImageTransform.Microsoft.Shadow(color=purple,
        direction=135);
    text-shadow: 0.1em 0.1em 0.05em purple;
    color:dodgerblue;
}
.redshadow {
    filter: progid:DXImageTransform.Microsoft.Shadow(color=red,
        direction=135);
    text-shadow: 0.1em 0.1em 0.05em red;
    color:white;
}
.glow {
    filter: progid:DXImageTransform.Microsoft.glow(Color=red,
        Strength=20);
    text-shadow: 0 0 0.2em red;
    color: white;
}
```

```
a:link {color: purple;}
a:visited {color: green;}
a:hover {color: red;}
a:active {color: blue;}
```

in index.html

```
<html style="height: 100%;">
```

```
<body class="gradient" style="font-family: Arial, Serif;
margin: 0 0 0 0;" bgcolor="yellow" text="blue">
    <h1 align="center" class="blueshadow">Our Home Page.</h1>
```

in ships.html

```
<ul style="background:palegreen;list-style-type: none;">
```

```
<h1 align="center" class="redshadow">Ships</h1>
```

in berserk.html

```
<h1 class="glow">Go berserk!!</h1>
```

Figure 82: Appendix code

F. TAKING THINGS FURTHER

If you want to see more CSS or HTML, try these web pages:
HTML: www.w3schools.com/html/default.asp
CSS: www.w3schools.com/css/default.asp

For more examples, ideas and pictures based on this book:
www.go-berserk.com

For Vikings, try these pages:
(they've been written in HTML and CSS)
www.vikinganswerlady.com
www.bbc.co.uk/schools/primaryhistory/vikings/

> **WRITE GOOD CODE (UNLIKE GOOGLE)**
> If you don't follow the HTML rules, your page may not show
> up properly. You can check your code at <u>validator.w3.org</u>.
> Unfortunately, many big web names failed the test -
> including Microsoft (14 mistakes), Yahoo (34 mistakes)
> and, bottom of the class, Google (50 mistakes).

Next, try our quiz!

Index

Here is a list of all the tags, all the parameters and all the important subjects in this book, as well as the pages they appear on:

Quiz

Here is a quiz based on all the fascinating facts in this book:

1. What is the most popular girl's name used for a password?

2. How many Germans love their Internet more than their girlfriend?

3. What is the reward for revealing the identity of the conficker virus's creator?

4. How many hours a day does the average teenager spend on multimedia?

5. What's the difference between the Internet and the World Wide Web?

6. In which country are all its citizens using the Internet?

7. Who invented HTML?

8. Who built the first web browser?

9. What is cybercrud?

10. What age is the youngest White Hat Hacker?

11. What is Mystery Meat Navigation?

12. What is the inventor of CSS called by his friends?

13. How many people have a CCIE certification?

14. Who invented Google cakes?

15. What colour is grey in older IE browsers?

16. What was the original name of Google?

17. What did the <blink> tag do?

18. How many people in the world go online?

19. What was the first word sent online?

20. What nationality is the first web surfer?

> **WHERE ARE THE HORNED HELMETS???**
> Vikings never wore horned helmets (until August Malmström painted his Viking pictures in 1850, http://enc.tfode.com/August_Malmstroem).
> But horned helmets were popular in Britain and Ireland.

> **NOTE**
> Get the answers from this book,
> and check them online at
> www.go-berserk.com.

You are now a web genius!!